I0532364

LIVING WITH PURPOSE

FIND YOUR PASSION | GROW YOUR INFLUENCE | MAXIMIZE YOUR ENDURANCE

JAMES JACKSON, III

SOUL EXCELLENCE PUBLISHING

PRAISE FOR JAMES JACKSON, III

"James Jackson's book *Living With Purpose* is a story in which people from many walks of life will be able to relate. His willingness to be vulnerable in sharing what held him back and what propelled him forward makes his story immensely relatable. At the same time, the constant pull - the passion - to build community is inspiring. James' story is a reminder that guided by a constancy of purpose we can experience accomplishments that may have otherwise seemed out of reach."

JENNIFER SMITH, CHIEF TECHNOLOGY & OPERATIONS OFFICER
ZIONS BANCORPORATION

"*Living With Purpose* is a deep dive into what it takes to really lead transformation in an ecosystem where there is an uneven playing field. James Jackson, III gives a "behind the scenes" look at his work and how he learned his true passion. I've been able to see James' work in action and it was great to read about the people, places, and experiences that shaped his leadership. As a bonus, his 'memoir-style' narrative provides a valuable history of the Black community in Utah."

SARA JONES, PRESIDENT, INCLUSIONPRO

"As a university president, one of my greatest hopes is that every student is able to discover their calling. I believe when you're passionate about the work you do, you're able to lead a more fulfilling life and make a greater impact in the world. But I often see students, recent graduates, and even working professionals struggle with discovering their "why." *Living WithPurpose* by James Jackson, III is a valuable guide for knowing where to begin. James shares his own account of what it took to break out of the rut of an unfulfilling career and arrive at a life filled with meaning and purpose.

James offers both practical advice and inspiring stories. He encourages readers to explore their passions and become involved in different organizations and projects. I especially appreciated his leadership lessons. James sets a powerful example through his perseverance through challenges and his drive to make a difference in his community. We can all learn from his commitment to personal growth. I highly recommend this book to anyone seeking to deepen their sense of purpose, create positive change in the world, and lead a more meaningful life."

TAYLOR RANDALL, PRESIDENT, UNIVERSITY OF UTAH

"James Jackson, III is the real deal—immensely talented, humble, witty, insightful, and most of all inspiring. It's a treat to read his personal story in his own words and to hear firsthand how he grew the Utah Black Chamber from an audacious idea into a Utah institution. The leadership and life lessons he shares in this book will inspire readers to find the passion that fuels their purpose, just as James has done."

STEPHANIE FROHMAN, SENIOR VICE PRESIDENT, STRATEGY &
PARTNERSHIPS ECONOMIC DEVELOPMENT CORPORATION
OF UTAH

"James has written a masterpiece on how to live and discover your purpose. The principles in this book will carry you higher."

RYAN WESTWOOD, TECHNOLOGY FOUNDER, ENTREPRENEUR,
AND INVESTOR

"Living With Purpose: Find Your Passion, Grow Your Influence, and Maximize Your Endurance is a captivating book that has impacted my perspective on life, passions, and purpose. Written with wisdom, passion, and insight, author James Jackson, III skillfully guides us through his own personal journey of exploration.

One of the book's strengths is James' ability to address the universal quest for passion, purpose, and motivation. It navigates the complexities of life with grace, offering tools and perspective for one's self to evolve. James' use of personal experience and antidotes fosters a sense of connection and encouragement.

I highly recommend this book to anyone, whether you're just starting your journey or have been in pursuit of passion for years."

LAURA STIREMAN, REGIONAL VICE PRESIDENT WCF
INSURANCE

"In a world where we are constantly bombarded with messages about success, achievement, and the pursuit of happiness, it can be easy to feel lost, overwhelmed, and uncertain about our own path in life. We are told to chase our dreams, find our passion, and live life to the fullest, but how do we do that? How do we unlock our own gifts and talents, and use them to make a meaningful impact in the world?

In *Living with Purpose,* James Jackson, III takes us on a personal journey of discovery, sharing his own story of how he found his purpose and ignited his passion. With honesty, vulnerability, and insight, he invites us to step into his world and learn from his experiences, offering practical advice and inspiration for anyone who is searching for their own path in life.

Through his words, we come to understand that purpose is not something that can be found overnight, but rather it is a journey of self-discovery that requires patience, perseverance, and a willingness to take risks. We learn that passion is not just a feeling, but a driving force that can help us overcome obstacles and stay committed to our goals. And we see that endurance is not just about gritting our teeth and soldiering on, but about finding the strength within ourselves to keep going even when the road ahead seems uncertain.

In short, *Living with Purpose* is a powerful reminder that we all have a story to tell and that our lives have the potential to make a lasting impact on the world. It is a book that will inspire readers to embrace their own journey, discover their purpose, and live life with intention and meaning. I highly recommend it to anyone who is seeking to find their own path in life, and to anyone who wants to be inspired by the courage and determination of one man's journey."

SANDRA HOLLINS, REPRESENTATIVE, STATE OF UTAH

"James is a builder. He has built a successful career. He has built a business. He builds community. He builds up others around him. With his new book, readers can easily discover and apply the lessons of 'building and creating purpose' that James has learned over a lifetime."

DEREK MILLER, PRESIDENT & CEO SALT LAKE CHAMBER

"With candor and heart, James Jackson, III shares his personal and professional journey and, in doing so, inspires readers to use their own strengths to achieve purpose in their lives. Throughout his story as a Salt Lake City native and active member of the local Black community, James demonstrates how we all can play roles in making our communities stronger for future generations."

SCOTT ANDERSON, PRESIDENT AND CEO ZIONS BANK

Print ISBN: 979-8-9883816-0-0

Ebook ISBN: 979-8-9883816-1-7

In memory of my Papa,

James Jackson, Sr.

1923 - 2012

Thank you for paving the way. I love and miss you.

CONTENTS

PART ONE
INTRODUCTION
1. Living with Purpose   3
2. The Village   15
3. Passion: The 'OG,' James Jackson, Sr.   23
4. Influence: Discovery   33
5. Endurance: The Process   45

PART TWO
THE WONDER YEARS
6. Passion: Waymon Tisdale III   57
7. Influence: Growing My Leadership   69
8. Endurance: It Was All A Dream   79

PART THREE
UTAH BLACK CHAMBER
9. In the Beginning   91
10. Passion: Every Day I'm Hustlin'   101
11. Influence: I Can Only Be Me   111
12. Endurance: Can't Stop, Won't Stop   125

PART FOUR
LEGACY
13. Passion: A Community Builder   143
14. Influence: The Next Episode   155
15. Endurance: Take Care of You   167

PART FIVE
CONCLUSION
16. Conclusion   185

Acknowledgments   193
Playlist   197
About the Author   199
Also by James Jackson, III   203
Notes   205

PART ONE
INTRODUCTION

1

LIVING WITH PURPOSE

"From what we get, we can make a living. What we give, however, makes a life."

– ARTHUR ASHE

LIFE IS ON PURPOSE. To live, we do many things purposefully, such as going to work and taking care of the family. Maybe we exercise, take vacations, and do activities to have fun. We do all of these things so that we can enjoy a happy and successful life. However, when was the last time you thought about why you are here? Why do you possess the gifts and talents that God gave you? You go out to earn an income in order to provide for yourself and your family. But what drives you to go out and earn that income? Why do you do what you do? Do you do it because it is something you can do? Do you do it because you're good at it, so you feel you have an opportunity to succeed? Do you do it because that's what you've always wanted to do since you were a kid? Or do you do it because it was the first or the most available thing out there, and you needed something?

Many of us will answer yes to one or more of these questions. However, have you paid attention to what drives you to go out and do the things you want to do? You want to be a provider, but that's not enough. Any opportunity can provide. A purpose comes from your passion. So, what are you passionate about?

I'm excited to take you on this journey of how I discovered my passion and began to live with a purpose. Through this journey, I hope that it helps you identify your purpose.

Who This Book Is For

• If you are struggling, trying to find a rhythm for your life

• If you're trying to discover your passion

• If you've hit a wall and looking for ways to push through

• If you've reached a peak, but know there's something more

• If you're looking to LIVE LIFE WITH PURPOSE

WHAT IS PASSION?

When I used to think of passion, I thought of someone displaying an intense action. But that's just the emotional reaction of passion. I love to watch sports. You see players displaying their passion all the time when they are playing the sport they love. It's easy to see their passion. At the beginning of the game, the captain or leader is ramping up their team with a chant displayed with loud movement. Their trash-talking is an example of passion for the game they love. You may not be able to hear them when the cameras show them shouting back and forth at each other, but you see that passion all over their faces. They celebrate or yell when they score or make a big play. They cry tears of sadness when they lose a big game and are overwhelmed with joy when they win a championship. You hear the saying, "They left it all on the field"' meaning the players gave the game everything they had in them to win. They used all of their talent, skills, heart, and emotions to win – their PASSION. They endured all they could to triumph. It's through their passion that you see their purpose. Their purpose in life is being that athlete.

I didn't think I was passionate about anything because I don't really display that kind of emotion. It's actually a little uncomfortable for me to do so. My personality is mostly laid back and chill. It's not that I lack emotion. Whether I am working, celebrating life, or enjoying any of my hobbies, I remain mostly even keel. During my involvement in network marketing, we started a cheer or chant for our team. I would yell, "We live!" and the team would respond back, "To dream big!" And we kept repeating it, trying to get louder and louder. When it was just us, I was fine, and it was fun. But when we were at a convention or event, I wasn't comfortable. I felt like it was forced. Was I *really* passionate? Financial independence was the mission and why I worked so hard for that company. On the surface, the commitment was there. I was at every meeting and convention. I was training other leaders in the company and held sales presentations throughout the state. Marketing tools could be found everywhere–at home, my car, and even at my full-time job. While shy and introverted, I tried getting out of my comfort zone and talking to as many people as I could about the service we offered. My belief was strong. The product I pushed I still use to this day. The success I had in that company, however, was only temporary. Eventually, when success wasn't coming, my commitment began to fizzle. Looking back now, I can confirm that I simply wasn't passionate. If I had been passionate, I would have managed through the rough times and found a way to succeed again. But when it got really hard and I didn't have a lot of money, my commitment to the process wasn't there, and I went back to the traditional working environment. I had the talent. I had the skills. I could do the work. I know I could have achieved success . . . only if I was passionate enough to do it. Passion would have pushed me through the tough times. It would have given me the courage and mental strength to find ways to push through the tough times. I've always believed there's a solution to every problem, and challenges don't come to defeat you. They come to promote you.

"I go to work to dig the ditch to make the money to buy the food to gain the strength to go back to work and dig the ditch."

– CHICAGO SANITATION WORKER

Do you feel this way at times or more often than you'd like? You go to a job you're not enjoying, but you need the money to live and provide for your family. However, when you get home, it needs attention as well: helping kids with homework, cooking, cleaning, yard work, and car maintenance. Does it feel like it never ends? Once your house is in order, you're tired, and you have just enough energy to sit on the couch and turn on the TV until it's time to go to bed. You say you want more. You know you can do more. You know you can become more, but just living can sometimes suck the energy out of you, leaving little for you to give to explore what 'more' looks like.

How do you find your way out of this vicious life cycle? There is something out there in the world that gives you purpose. There is something out there in the world that will light a fire under you. You were not meant to just live. You are here to have life and have it abundantly. Your time here is on purpose. Finding your purpose should be intentional. I wouldn't recommend allowing it to reveal itself on its own. If you feel stuck in the repetitive life like the Chicago sanitation worker, you may never allow it to come to pass. John Maxwell said, "Your potential is God's gift to you. Using your potential is your gift back to Him." Don't allow yourself to pass through life with the gifts and talents that you have been given.

FINDING MY PURPOSE

Once my grandfather introduced me to my strengths of public speaking, I was on a mission to find my purpose. My success in delivering church speeches gave me the perspective I needed to know that I have purpose, and I should seek to find what it is. It took me longer than I anticipated, but once I found it, living life has never been the same. I am not a millionaire. I don't own a fancy house or houses in different locations. While I won't say "no" to those fun things once I am in a position to acquire them, I have found happiness. Happiness to me is having purpose in life. Knowing that, I know I will have those things eventually. Material things don't give me purpose. They are the results of living with purpose. One of my mentors shared, "become a millionaire not for the money, but for the person you will become."

When you live with purpose, an alarm clock doesn't wake you up. It is simply there to keep you on task. Your purpose wakes you up. You are up with a hunger for life. You have things you have to do, tasks you have to accomplish, and people you have to meet.

When you live with purpose, home is a sanctuary for you to recharge, recalibrate, and recover instead of a place to dwell, disassociate, and die.

When you live with purpose, your career or business is purposeful. You have a mission to deliver impact in a way that lasts beyond your lifetime, leaving a legacy for you and your family.

FINDING MY PASSION

The light came on for me several years into building the Utah Black Chamber. Once I began to feel more comfortable in the environment I was creating, I began to identify stronger leaders on the board and improve our strategy to connect to the community. My "swag" began to change. I knew how the chamber could impact the community. It wasn't just about having a successful organization in Utah. It wasn't just about having a successful "Black" organization in Utah. It was about the impact. My vision grew bigger and my passion became stronger. The chamber was a vehicle to help make that impact.

After realizing my passion, I realized I was using the same skills, abilities, and even experiences I had in networking marketing. I wasn't successful because I was just in the wrong vehicle, so the passion wasn't there. Often we think we don't have the talent required to fulfill our dreams based on our past experiences. However, sometimes it could be because we were just in the wrong vehicle. When I was leading the Black Chamber, I was selling memberships, promoting events, and continuously sharing the vision. When I was in networking marketing, I was selling memberships, promoting events, and continuously sharing the vision. For a couple of years, I was working with both organizations. Why was I succeeding in the Black Chamber and not the networking marketing company if I was using the same skills? I was in the wrong vehicle. The passion wasn't in network marketing. I found passion in the chamber. And when you find passion, you'll find peace and comfort in your ability to succeed and you'll even improve those skills now that you're working in the right vehicle.

The Utah Black Chamber introduced me to my purpose. I went on this journey of learning more about myself, my leadership, my talents, skills, and abilities and used them towards my purpose of bringing change to this world. This book shares with you how I have lived with purpose once I found my passion. Through the many obstacles, challenges and barriers life brought me, I have preserved and kept growing. My purpose showed me what I needed to do to grow my influence. I learned the most important ability to grow in life is leadership. Growing up, I never saw myself as a leader, and now I consider myself an influencer in my community and am working to continue to expand my influence far and wide. To keep growing, my endurance was definitely tested–mentally, emotionally, physically, and spiritually. I had to develop routines to keep myself focused, resilient, and strong.

After writing the book _Black Utah: Stories from the Thriving Community_, I felt it was time to share my story. I interviewed dozens of people who shared their stories and experiences but didn't share much about myself. I've always remained humble in my growth journey, but I felt it was time to share who I am and how I came to be today. I want to inspire others who are looking for a path for themselves. I want to help people learn how they can find their passion, grow their influence, and maximize their endurance to pursue their purpose in life.

DEFINE PASSION FOR YOU

Passion is the fuel to help you find your purpose. Having a life with no passion is not really living. You're just going through the day-to-day trying to survive instead of living to thrive. This is where I was before I started the chamber. I didn't like the feeling. For a little time, while being down on myself, I understood how people can live in that state. With no purpose. No passion. Uninspired. It's not the way to live. Sometimes, we can get sucked into a mundane life. We just focus on taking care of our family, household bills, and the happiness of life. However, it's just not enough. If that's just our focus, that flame can go out quickly.

"There was a very cautious man who never laughed or played.

He never risked, he never tried, he never sang or prayed.

And one day when he passed away, his insurance was denied.

For since he never really lived, they claimed he never really died."

– DENIS WAITLEY

Are you someone who is struggling to find your purpose? What are you passionate about? What do you want for your family? What lengths are you willing to go to commit to your family? Do you want to become a better spouse or partner? Find your passion. Do you want to be the best parent a child can have? Find your passion. If you want to be the best provider, supporter, and motivator? Find your passion. You don't want to become that "cautious man" described above. You have been blessed with certain gifts, talents and are going through experiences to become something great. Once you find your purpose, your passion will carry you through and bring you success.

"If you do what you love and love what you do, you will never work a day in your life."

–BRANDYN GUNDY

What is passion? Passion is your alarm clock to get you up in the morning. Not just rise, but it'll get you up even when you don't want to. If that bed is too comfy or it's the weekend, and you just want to sleep in, you know what you have to do to get to where you want to be. "Do today what others don't, so you'll have tomorrow what others won't." Yes, you do want family time and "me time," but your passion will motivate you to carve out time out of your schedule to find more time in the morning or late at night to work towards your goal.

What is passion? When you speak about it, people see you light up. There is a spark big enough to not only light a fire within you but inspire people around you. Have you ever heard a pastor preach and you feel the spirit inside of you? Or any inspiring speaker delivering a message and you feel something inside of you? You feel inspired, motivated, encouraged, or emotional about your circumstances. You are excited for change. You are feeling their passion. Passion inspires. Passion elevates. Passion makes you feel like you can conquer anything.

What is passion? Passion is the fuel you need to carry out your purpose. You can't achieve your purpose without passion, and passion doesn't exist without a sense of purpose. They go hand in hand. If you haven't found your passion, find it. Start paying attention to what lights you up. What would you fight for? What is your heart telling you? What would get you up in the morning if you could have it every day? Take time to think about these questions before moving to the next chapter. Life is meaningless without passion. But once you find it, you'll discover the life you've always wanted.

"If you can't figure out your purpose, figure out your passion. For your passion will lead you right to your purpose."

– TD JAKES

How do you find your passion? Passion comes with the right vehicle. You have to be willing to look beyond what life gives you, and you give to life. It may come with your willingness to change, step outside your comfort zone, and realize you may just be in the wrong vehicle. Don't allow your gifts, talents, and skills to go without purpose. You belong on this earth to do something great.

Thank you for taking the time to read about my journey to finding my purpose and what purpose means to me. I'm still on my journey, not finding my passion, but the journey of using my passion towards my purpose and delivering maximum impact before I leave this earth. This is my story. I believe we all have a story to tell to inspire others. I hope you find it inspiring and encouraging for you to discover and live the life you've always imagined it to be.

THE VILLAGE

"It takes a village to raise a child."

– AFRICAN PROVERB

MY CHILDHOOD SEEMS PRETTY NORMAL. I had loving parents and an extended family that supported me. My parents were young when I was born, 18 and 20 years old. They had a lot of support from family and the church community. I grew up in a church surrounded by mentors and influencers. Calvary Baptist Church is the oldest Black Baptist church in Utah – four years older than Utah's statehood. It has always maintained itself as a community hub for Black Utah. My parents provided me with a typical childhood, both working to provide for my sister and me. My Dad has always worked in construction, from general construction to electrician and property management. My mom has only had two jobs since I have known her, first working with medical supplies and then moving to quality assurance for large industrial pumps. One thing my parents have always given my sister and me was consistency. We never experienced any major bumps in the road. Even when they had their own challenges in life and/or work, they made sure it never impacted us. I attended public school, had friends, received good grades, and was able to attend college. I never thought about how much my childhood had an impact on who I have become. I thought it was the beginning of my career, being exposed to challenges and opportunities, that opened my eyes. However, looking back, it was my village that shaped my response to those challenges and opportunities.

FINDING MY IDENTITY

I was born and raised in Salt Lake City, Utah. I am always prepared for the response when people hear that, whether I'm traveling throughout the country or even just conversing with people here, as this state has become more and more of a hot spot for people to relocate. Utah is known as a predominantly white state with a dominant religion. The second president of the Church of Jesus Christ of Latter Day Saints, Brigham Young, led his followers from Nauvoo, Illinois to the Salt Lake Valley in 1847. The territory was established as "This is the Place," and Utah became the base of that church. The Latter Day Saint Pioneers that arrived with Young were mostly white, and there were a few notable slaves – Hark Lay, Oscar Crosby, and Green Flake. However, the majority of the growth of Utah's Black population began with the railroad jobs, as those jobs were the best-paying jobs for Blacks and minorities during the late 1800s and early 1900s, and the military, as there were two or three military bases of the buffalo soldiers. The Black population still didn't exceed one percent until after 2010 and has never been above two percent, despite the state's growth. With that said people don't think about a Black person living here, staying here, or even being born here!

Not only was I born here, but I am also second-generation. Both pairs of my grandparents relocated to Utah in the mid-1950s. My maternal grandparents are Mexican, originally from McAllen, Texas, a small city on the border of Texas and Mexico. Most people don't recognize my Hispanic side, mostly because I was raised around my African-American heritage. However, when I was growing up, I always wanted to represent both sides. I love both sides of my family, and I have been fortunate to have both close to me and remain connected to this day. For me, being bi-racial was challenging. I wanted people to know who I was wholly. There were times I felt guilty when I didn't represent my Hispanic side well enough. I learned Spanish in school but never became fluent. I became more engaged with Black history than Mexican history. As I got older, I realized it was not realistic to constantly represent both. My influence came from who I was most influenced by, and being raised in a Black Baptist church, I connected more with my African-American side. Also, society will drive you to affiliate more with one over the other by how they see you. If you look Black, you will be treated as a Black person. When Barack Obama was President of the United States, rarely was there any mention of his white heritage. As a matter of fact, some people were convinced that President Obama was born in Africa! There are many other examples of entertainers and influencers who are only recognized by their dominant race or ethnicity, and just a handful of examples where both are mildly celebrated. Our Vice President of the United States, Kamala Harris, was recognized publicly for not only being the first Black and female Vice President, but also the first Indian

Vice President. NBA player, Jordan Clarkson, has been able to represent his Asian heritage during certain celebrations such as Asian Heritage Month or play for the Filipino national basketball team. One of the most successful professional golfers in history, Tiger Woods, is recognized as being Black, but his mother is from Thailand.

If society sees you as Black, you're Black. You're going to be treated as Black in every aspect of life, good and bad. The best thing I could do is own my Blackness and represent the community the best way I can. I give credit to my parents for surrounding me with people who not only influenced me but also protected me. Growing up in a predominantly white state, you are met with very fascinating experiences. When people are not familiar with a particular race or culture, they relate to what they see and hear in the media and respond accordingly. I encountered more ignorance than racism. I was grateful for my church home because it was not only a place with people who I could better relate with, but it was also a safe place for me, and I was able to share my experiences with my peers, and we would talk about how each other responded to certain circumstances.

For example, the most popular experience most of us had was people wanting to feel our hair (when I had hair) like we were a pet. From junior high to early adulthood, I had finger waves. I loved my waves. I would use a special pomade like Sportin Waves or American Crew for my hair and would wear my durag overnight while sleeping to form my waves. My barber had the same hair as me, and he would taper my fade just right and give the best lineup. We all have different hairstyles. However, because of the texture of a Black person's hair, people have this desire to feel it, and it does make us feel like some kind of pet.

Sometimes, people would just come up and touch my hair without even asking, including people I barely know.

Our body responds to the climate differently than white people, and some people would comment about our different shades of skin. Or they would assume that we are great singers and athletes. They think we all know each other (however, it could be likely given the small population in Utah, but still. . .) Sometimes white people would want to try to "speak like us" in order to try to connect with us. They would greet me, saying, "What's up, bro?" Or want to give me what they would think would be a "Black-like" handshake, although they wouldn't greet others like that. Sometimes, people would wonder why I don't speak "Black," like we spoke a different language or something. As a child, it was sometimes exhausting to be Black in Utah, trying to navigate these experiences the best way I could. For most of my formal education, I was one of just a handful Black students. I was the only Black student in the entire elementary school until fifth grade, when four more came. In junior high school, the Black population of students doubled and then doubled again by high school. It wasn't until college that I saw a large enough Black student body in my school to help make school life a little more comfortable for me but likely had no intention of staying once they finished school. I would hang out with many of them, mostly athletes, during lunchtime in the university cafeteria. Many of the friends I connected with at my church left Utah after high school for college to seek more diverse environments. They just couldn't handle this environment anymore. I didn't blame them for leaving, but college was free for me if I attended the University of Utah. Most of my family was in Utah as well, so what would be more challenging, being away from family or remaining in Utah or dealing with what I was dealing with and hoping for change?

THE VILLAGE IMPACT

As I got older, I realized that my upbringing was different from many young Black males around the country. I could be jealous of people from predominantly Black neighborhoods, but unfortunately, most of those neighborhoods are low-income. According to research, the median household income of Black Americans is about $45,000, 30% less than white households, with single households being significantly less than that. A shocking 70% of the nation's majority-Black zip codes are considered distressed, meaning that there is widespread poverty, high levels of unemployment, and low levels of educational attainment.[1] When I recognized this, I thought about what I would rather encounter more: being surrounded by mostly Black people, so I would feel better connected, but potentially living in an unsafe environment with influences that could potentially lead me to "Chicago Sanitation Worker" lifestyle or worse, or live in a predominantly white neighborhood and encounter ignorance and a little bit of racism, but that is about as unsafe as it gets? While neither sounds optimal, my village was equipped with people who have had a significant impact on my life, directly and indirectly.

I wasn't an outgoing person when I was young. I was quite the opposite–quiet and shy. Many people may not even know they impacted me, but I watched and observed individuals who inspired me and significantly influenced who I am today. Within my church, I grew up around business owners, educators, and successful professionals, in addition to clergy people. In predominantly Black neighborhoods in other parts of the country, individuals may have had a really different set of influencers, so I consider myself very fortunate to be surrounded by individuals who were not only successful but also worked to lift their community through activism, volunteering, leading nonprofit organizations and community events, and working with our youth. I felt like everyone around me had a vested interest in my success, and I didn't want to let them down. Yet I knew I would be picked up if I failed, celebrated when I succeeded and supported throughout my journey whenever I needed it. The only person who would hold me back was me.

Because of this village, I got comfortable in my environment. While many of my friends wanted something more out of their community, like a social environment full of diversity, I wasn't ready to expand outside of my comfort zone. Most of my family was here, I had a good church home, and even though school wasn't as diverse as my church, I managed through, receiving grades good enough to get scholarships to college. One of the scholarships I received that surprised me was a leadership scholarship. I never led anything, so I don't know what or how this happened in the beginning. It wasn't until it was closer to school starting that I found out it was someone from my village. It's not always about being the loudest or the most popular. Sometimes, it's the individual who's quietly focused, implementing lessons learned, committing to his mentors, and moving with ambition. From that scholarship, I received a full-ride to the University's business school, and I earned degrees in Marketing and Finance. I always wanted to be a businessman. I just didn't know exactly where in business I wanted to work. But the path for me seemed to have been settled. I didn't have strong enough reasons to leave Utah. I felt comfortable enough to remain here, staying with my family and committed to the village that raised me. I knew I would have success if I stayed here with this support surrounding me. However, I still didn't have a clear path or understand my purpose. What opportunities would I take advantage of here?

REFLECTION

What does your village look like? Who are you influenced by? I've been taught that we are most influenced by the five people we hang around with the most. You may have heard of the phrase, "Birds of a feather flock together" or something similar. As you think of the influencers in your life, how are they leading you?

PASSION: THE 'OG', JAMES JACKSON, SR.

"Every dream begins with a dreamer. Always remember, you have within you the strength, the patience, and the passion to reach for the stars to change the world."

– HARRIET TUBMAN

JAMES JACKSON, SR., OR "PAPA," was my primary inspiration for who I am today. He and my grandmother, Ida Mae, arrived in Salt Lake City from Muskogee, Oklahoma, in the 1950s. They were on their way to visit a relative in California but heard about the job opportunities here in Utah. Papa began working at the Tooele Army Depot, but I mostly remember him working at the University of Utah, managing one of the custodial teams. He led many of the custodian teams there throughout his 40-year career. When I attended the university for my undergraduate degrees, I always sought him out in the cafeteria building to catch up for lunch or just to say hello. He always bragged about me to colleagues, which made me want to continue to make him proud.

I loved listening to his stories, and he was always a jokester. He loved to have fun. From colleagues and church members to even servers at restaurants, people will always remember his smile and playfulness. He never shared much with me about how challenging it was for him and Nana. I'm sure he would have told me if I asked, though. He had only an elementary school education, and he and Nana raised four children together, rarely showing any signs of struggle. They lived modestly and always made sure they were able to provide necessities, helping family members from children, grandchildren, and even great-grand-children. At times, I felt like it was a challenge for me to make him proud, though. Nana and Papa were pretty orthodox in their Baptist ways, and they always were well-dressed. Papa wore a suit every day to work, sometimes even a three-piece suit. He wore a suit even at home, with no plans to go anywhere. They attended church every Sunday, including Sunday school and special afternoon services. Papa was in the Laymen ministry, the male chorus, and a deacon, and Nana was in the women's mission, a deaconess, and mass choir member. I knew if I was spending time with them on the weekend, it was church all the time. I didn't mind it much because I just loved hanging out with them. Also, I felt like I could "be fully Black" around them and at church, not feeling a need to "code-switch" in an attempt to connect with my white peers at school.

Nana always fed me so well. I loved her cooking. She turned me on to collard greens and pound cake. She grew her own greens in her garden, and that's the only thing I remembered that she had in her garden. My favorite days are when we would have family get-togethers at their house with Nana's cooking and

Papa on the charcoal BBQ grill, and we would play cards or dominoes. I never wanted to leave. I have yet to find anyone that prepared greens and pound cake as well as she did. If it wasn't gospel music, it was BB King or any other jazz they listened to. I was always nervous about bringing any friends or girlfriends around. I was scared to know if they would meet their standards. Usually, their first question was if they were church-going people. I was nervous my friends would do or say something that wouldn't meet their approval. One year, I grew my hair out to be braided into cornrows and had my ears pierced. They never let that down. That was the one season where I had disappointed them the most. They couldn't believe their grandson would want to present himself that way. Even after I cut my hair back down and stopped wearing earrings (one of the attire requirements for an internship I took restricted earrings for men), they would often bring it up and share how that was not a good look for me from their perspective and that they were so happy that I decided to get rid of that look.

THE ROADMASTER

I traveled with them to several church conventions around the country. They hated flying, so we drove everywhere. They owned a red Buick Roadmaster, and they put that name to the test. I would guess they visited or traveled through nearly every state in the country in that car. Seattle, Los Angeles, Phoenix, and St. Louis are some of the places I can remember traveling to with them. There were opportunities to travel further east and south, but that didn't pan out. I didn't mind road trips with them. I liked getting the atlas or a map and following along where we were going. This was pre-GPS, of course. I would look forward to seeing the landmarks that were marked on the map.

Papa was always entertaining on these trips. I have so many memories of Papa joking around with the server at restaurants, talking about how rich he was with his little coin purse, or telling me it was time to go play outside when the food was ready. Nana and Papa's laughs and personalities were infectious, especially when Nana was having a good laugh. She would squeal so loud, and you couldn't help but to laugh along with her, even if you didn't know what she was laughing about.

Nana and Papa passed away in 2014 and 2012, respectively, each living to be almost 90 years old. Both of their birthdays were around Memorial Day weekend, and we used to have a family BBQ on Memorial Day in the park to celebrate. We continued to get together for Memorial Day even after they passed to honor them. I have so many memories of them, and I know I learned so much from them. One of my favorite pastimes was playing dominoes with Papa and my dad. How he played, you would never know he only had an elementary school education. He was so sharp and witty. I credit Papa for how I dress, my humor, and my love for family. He would go out of his way to help anyone in his family. He would make you feel like he had all the resources in the world.

PASSION FOUND BEHIND THE PODIUM

It was Papa who inspired me to become an inspirational speaker. During the winter of 1992, when I was 12 years old, Papa asked me if I would be interested in going with him to Los Angeles for a church convention the following spring. They were looking for youth speakers and wanted to know if I was interested. I loved Papa so much that it was hard to say no to him. I had given Easter and Christmas speeches at church, but nothing like what he was asking. I never thought about giving speeches outside of those church holiday speeches. I was too shy to do any more than that. But I guess he didn't see me as quiet and shy; perhaps in a different light, he saw me as smart and well-spoken. So I agreed.

I found a topic and went to work. Nana gave me a huge study Bible, and I used that to help me write my speech. After a little reading and homework, I found a verse that related to the theme of the convention and found other verses to support my speech. The whole process reminded me of school and working on an essay. I took some pointers from sermons I have heard ministers preach to help me with the outline – the opening, structuring my objectives, and a strong closing. To this day, I still remember what Bible verse my speech was based on, Proverbs 3:5-6. These are the first verses I committed to memory and became my favorite Bible passage:

"Trust in the Lord with all your heart and lean not on your own understanding. Believe in him and He will make your paths straight."

– PROVERBS 3: 5-6

A few days before we left for the convention, Papa and I had dinner with a few other Laymen members of the church at a Pizza Hut (back when they had a salad buffet) to discuss logistics. I was nervous about missing school because a test was scheduled for the Monday following the convention, so they were planning how to get me back home. This would be the first time I would fly on a plane, and I flew back by myself. During that Pizza Hut dinner, I shared my topic with the group. They were delighted and couldn't wait to hear it. That support boosted my confidence. Papa was excited for me, and I didn't realize where this experience would end up taking me. It shifted my perception of what I thought about myself. I discovered this ability I unknowingly possessed, and I enjoyed it.

On the first day of the convention, thirty years ago now, I delivered my speech to several hundred people, mostly elderly Black men, at a Baptist Laymen conference. I remember being the first part of the convention in the morning, so I am thankful I am a morning person. I don't remember being nervous. All I remember was wanting to make Papa proud. My grandfather beamed with pride, and I felt like a star of the show the rest of the convention. People kept coming up to me, sharing how amazing a job I did and how much of a natural I was. Some even thought a career as a Baptist preacher was in my future. Behind that podium, I went from a shy young boy to a confident presenter hoping to inspire others.

After returning home, I received more speaking opportunities within the church and the broader Baptist church community. Word spread of how well I did at the convention. I spoke at regular church services, holiday services, conferences and events, and even a speech contest with a monetary prize! I was really excited about that one because, as far as I knew, there weren't too many other people my age who were speaking in churches as often as me. There was another gentleman, a little bit older, who humbled me though. He gave a great talk with energy and had people shouting in response to his message. He ended up winning the contest, but we also became friends for a while. It was good to know there were other young men within our community churches who people could call on for church services.

One of my most memorable speeches was during a regular service at my church. After I presented, a young man came to the front of the church to accept the calling of becoming a Christian during the altar call part of the service. He shared his struggles and wanting to do better and was moved by my message and ready to become a Christian. After he shared his testimony, I walked up to him and gave him a hug. While we embraced, he shared his appreciation and was so happy he had come that Sunday. He felt it was a sign for him to come and listen to someone his age share that kind of passion for Christ. That moment is what really changed the trajectory for me whenever I was in the front of the room. For the first speech I gave for Papa, my aim was to make him proud and show the people in the room who his grandson was. After that moment when that young gentleman made a life decision because of the message I gave, I felt that was the kind of impact I wanted to make every time I give a speech. In church or outside of it, I wanted to inspire. I wanted to touch someone through my message. Whether I speak for five minutes or an eight-hour training session, my main goal is always to inspire, whether I touch just one person or more. I don't want to be on stage just to be in the spotlight. If I'm given the opportunity, I'm coming with it! I don't speak to boast, gloat, or perform. I intend to deliver with a purpose in mind. This is why I don't consider myself a motivational speaker, but an inspirational speaker.

Speaking at church functions so often made me feel comfortable enough to accept a role in a high school play. I was asked if I would play the role of "Crooks" in Mice of Men. Since there were very few Black students at my high school, the theater department hoped that I would accept the opportunity so they could do this play. This was my first time going into the secular community with my speaking abilities, so I was a little nervous. I had never done a play before and had to memorize a lot of pages of lines, but I found my groove over time. I was in physical therapy to rehabilitate my knee from an injury, so I worked on my lines while I was lying on the bed with a massage machine connected to my knee. It only took opening night for me to be comfortable. Apparently, I just needed an audience to produce the strength and energy for me to perform. I invited my whole family to come see me. It felt natural to me. This was an opportunity to be a person other than myself, and I took advantage of it. The other actors praised the performance I gave and were grateful I had accepted the role. They were amazed I had never acted before and thought they would see me more in acting classes. Our school became state champions from that play, using some of the scenes I played in. This experience gave me more confidence, adding to my skill set and knowing I could expand my speaking ability beyond church functions. Many song artists I grew up listening to and some I listen to today had their beginnings in the church, and I was taking the same path. Just not singing or playing an instrument. There was a small moment of time when I thought acting could be in my future, but I ended up not following through on that path. My shyness overpowered my interest in pursuing acting. Maybe if I had had closer friends who were thespians, I would have tried it out, but I chose not to change my school schedule. Looking back, it probably could have benefited me. I have done several television interviews and PSA television ads these past few years. While people said I was a natural, I wonder if there could have been opportunities to be in television professionally.

SPEAKING FOR PAY

My first paid speaking gig came from a church event. A special Baptist conference of several local churches was being held at a local downtown hotel. Papa reached out and asked if I would be one of the speakers. I was already in college at the time, doing what college kids do. Those "activities" distracted me from this skill I was developing, but I was being introduced to new people and experiences. Because of that, I hadn't spoken at a church event in a while, but since it was Papa who was asking, I couldn't say no. It felt different to me this time. Maybe because I was older, and this event was at a hotel in my hometown instead of out of state. I recognized many of the faces in the room, and I was a little nervous.

The speech in Los Angeles was raw and exciting, and I was ready to impress, but this time it felt almost obligatory and a little dull. Honestly, it wasn't my best performance. The energy was totally different, and I was a little disappointed in the applause I received when I finished. It wasn't the same energy I had experienced before. Maybe because I wasn't a young teenager anymore, but it was a reminder of how much I enjoyed presenting in front of a room of people to inspire them in some way. I could tell it had been a while since my grandparents had seen me in that light because I had never seen them that emotional after hearing me speak. Seeing their faces brought me back to the foundation of my growth. I knew public speaking was a skill I should never let go of. After the event, one of the church leaders found me, and I thought they were going to ask me to speak at another service, but he wanted to give me an envelope. It was a check for $100! I didn't even know I was getting paid. I got paid $100 for a 15-minute presentation. If I had known that, I probably would have prepared better! I had a couple more paid speaking opportunities at church events, and it got me thinking, "Could I have a career doing this?"

REFLECTION

Influencers can be the primary source to introduce you to your passion or even your purpose. They are the ones who are most likely to see something in you that you haven't. In the last chapter, I asked you to think about the influencers in your life. If you are struggling to find something you're passionate about, maybe connect with one of them for a conversation about helping you see more about yourself. You may be surprised by what they have to share with you.

4

INFLUENCE: DISCOVERY

"Success is to be measured not so much by the position that one has reached in life as by the obstacles which he has overcome while trying to succeed."

– BOOKER T. WASHINGTON

AFTER GIVING many church speeches in my teens and throughout high school and engaging more in church ministries and activities, several people in my church predicted that I would become the next pastor of Calvary Baptist Church. While I was becoming very versed in the Bible, it was initially because of the preparation for the topics for my speech. Listening to many sermons given by my pastor and other ministers, I would pay attention to how they would find other Bible verses that would support their topic and objectives. They would provide short stories and anecdotes from their own experiences or others. I took styles from different preachers and created my own kind of delivery. I did become a stronger Christian by giving these speeches. I also realized God had provided me with a voice for a reason and designed a path for me to use this voice. Being a pastor of a church, though, was not that path. It did spark a thought, though, *Who am I going to become?* I felt I had to have a role where my voice was in front of an audience since I enjoyed it so much. I didn't see myself as an activist like Martin Luther King, Jr.. All I knew at the time was that my public speaking was going to be in a community environment. That's where I felt I would be most comfortable, presenting to the village that has always supported me. I never thought that I would be doing it in a corporate environment. For some reason, I didn't see my speaking style to be in a stiff corporate world. I wanted to inspire, make an impact, and get people moving toward a purpose or goal.

Throughout college, I participated in many organizations and projects where I lent my thoughts and sometimes my voice. Whether it was the Black Student Union or the NAACP College Chapter, I played somewhat of a leadership role. I began to learn about all the different community organizations the Black community had in Utah and realized we were a lot bigger and a lot closer than I thought we were. Most people knew what others were doing, and there was a sense of support for one another, particularly when it related to our youth. Through these channels, I began to find my path. I spoke at a few community functions and sometimes banquets. Using the same style I had for church speeches, I tweaked it so it was a little more secular, so my speech could relate to a larger audience. It did take more effort since the base for all of my speeches was in church, so I had to learn how to share more of my own experiences and research other anecdotes. I used stories from Black leaders throughout history and even some information I learned from watching television. I kept looking for things that could inspire people and tried to keep my style consistent. People knew who my grandparents were. People knew who my mom and dad were. My dad played bass guitar for many of the choirs in the church and was often called on to guest play in the church community. Now, people were beginning to know who I was. The third generation, James Jackson. I was becoming my own self rather than Brother Jackson's grandson or Cameron's boy (my dad's and my middle name). I started developing my own brand. Was this the leader that people saw while I was growing up?

CHURCH > COMMUNITY > CORPORATE

Living in Utah, it was only a matter of time before I was exposed to the network marketing industry. Utah is a home for many network marketing company headquarters. When I was young, my dad was a representative for Amway and Melaleuca for several years. I didn't understand it at the time. I hated the products that we used. I didn't mind the hygiene products as much as the food. He tried to tell me the cereal was the same as the name brands, but I could taste the difference! It wasn't until I was introduced to the business side of network marketing that I understood why network marketing was so attractive. The pitch was simple: make an extra $500-$1,000 a month working part-time from home. Eventually, that could lead to a full-time income and work any time you want while earning a passive income. Why not try it? I started the journey at the young age of 22, just out of college. I just started working in what I thought would be my full-time career in finance at Morgan Stanley. This was another part of my life that changed my thinking forever. In network marketing, I learned the benefits of being an entrepreneur and earning multiple streams of income. I was introduced to the abilities of leadership and growing people. Reading personal development books became a hobby of mine, and I was excited about the growth I was experiencing, more mentally than the income.

I joined the company in a partnership with a high school friend. He started a business and reached out to me to help him. To this day, I am still not exactly sure what our business did, but the main purpose was to help businesses grow, and he had resources such as web development and graphic design to support businesses. He was hoping my college-degreed finance brain could help him. Little did we both know that it takes more of an entrepreneurial mindset than the formal educational back-ground I had to grow a successful business. We really had no idea what we were doing with his business, but we acted like we did! The experience was necessary for my journey, though.

One day, a neighbor came to his door to welcome him to the neighborhood he just moved into. She asked about his profes-sion, and after learning about him, she invited him to a business meeting to learn about what she was doing and potentially find customers for his business. That's how she got us. We were desperate to find customers, so we were down to try anything. We arrived a little late, and the presenter was already giving his presentation. It was what you would expect at one of these meetings. Someone at the front dressed very sharply, sharing the need for their product, but mostly selling the opportunity to become a sales associate of their business. When the presenta-tion was finished, the neighbor introduced us to the presenter, and we shared more about ourselves and our business. He kindly acknowledged our business and asked us to consider how the services this company offered could be incorporated into our business model. The recommendation didn't sound too bad for us, so we decided to take a look at this company more. Both the neighbor and the presenter introduced us to the presenter's older brother, who lived just up the street from my friend. He also was in the business and was very successful. The house he lived in was about triple the size of the house I grew up in, and we met in his large home office. He went over everything in detail about the product and the business, sharing how to maximize our income with the compensation plan. Of course, our young, hungry eyes lit up, and we thought this could be pretty exciting.

We agreed with what they proposed and incorporated the networking marketing business into the business we were running together and signed up our business as the sales associate for the network marketing company. We thought he would be the salesman and I would be the operations guy. He was a lot more outgoing than I was. He was popular at school, and when we got older, he started in the entertainment industry, acting in films and commercials and singing. We seemed like a great dynamic duo at the time. As we were still trying to figure out our business, we began seeing faster results from the networking marketing business. We were moving up in the business pretty quickly. We had a lot of support from the network marketing leaders locally, and they took a liking to the energy we gave to the weekly meetings and events. We were attracting more diversity as the two young Black men with different circles of influence. Eventually, the network marketing business became more exciting, and we focused more of our efforts on building the business there than what the business was originally intended.

We made it to the top bonus level of the company and we had salespeople all across the country and even a couple in Canada. Our team was hosting weekly home meetings, and we would go to the homes to do the presentation for them. During the national conventions, we would have a small group from our team to attend along with us, sparking more growth within our organization every year. My dad even joined our organization and was having a little bit of success. He stayed in the business longer than I did. In the first few years, it seemed like this was going to be our path to financial freedom. I thought in a couple of years, I could leave my full time job. Our charisma and approach to the business attracted the local leaders of the company, and we began leading the weekly events held in our area. I found myself back in the speaking realm again, this time giving sales presentations and training. What was fascinating was that I was closing other people's sales more than my own. People loved when I was presenting. I began to feel like an imposter, though. Usually, it was the successful associates of the business presenting, who were earning a full-time income doing this business. I wasn't anywhere near that level. Leadership didn't care, though. There was a small circle of presenters, and it was good to put new faces in there to mix it up. Besides, I would be working this business full-time eventually, right?

People loved the energy I had when I presented. Once again, I used the same style I had developed by giving church presentations, but now I was more developed. I had a different genre of presenters I was listening to; I was reading books on personal growth and was attending their conferences, and listening to their CDs. I found myself attracted to the styles of standup comedians. While their whole purpose is to make people laugh, I realized the foundation of their delivery was no different than a preacher, a motivational speaker, or a sales presenter. The same elements were still there, but a comedian engages the audience differently. I felt adding some humor into my presentations would elevate my game. As a result, I was one of the most requested speakers locally. I was delivering a presentation at least once a month and traveled up and down the state of Utah. I was even invited to give home presentations for other teams. Over time, though, the imposter feeling was taking over. I began feeling like a hypocrite when talking about the opportunity, especially when the business for us began to slow down. I could deliver an awesome presentation, but I was struggling with my own business. My friend was the better salesperson, and I leaned on him more than I should have to carry the production. That was the deal in the beginning, but as our team grew, I had to figure out a way to step up. I had to help our team close sales. I had to show them how the business worked and take them out to do sales calls. It was a wake-up call for me. In order for me to truly be a leader, I had to be the example. I couldn't just lead by putting on a show in front of the room. The feeling of not being able to have my own success in this company wasn't good, and it began to wear me down.

This was part of my life for nearly ten years. Most of our production came in the first few years, and we spent more than half of the time trying to keep our team intact and find other ways to grow the business. My friend and I both experienced life changes and challenges that hurt our momentum. Once we lost momentum, it was hard to get it back. I stayed in it longer than I should have, but I was so grateful for the personal growth opportunities it provided me. I learned about myself as a leader and a business person. My eyes were opened to more than just the corporate world for earning an income. When our organization started to slow and production was waning, I felt it was me who was eventually our demise. Leadership guru, John Maxwell, says, "Everything rises and falls on leadership." I knew I could become a better leader and even a better public speaker with the right vehicle. Even though network marketing didn't work out to become the vehicle, it prepared me for the right one when it came along.

BECOMING A JOHN MAXWELL TEAM MEMBER

After my time in network marketing, I still wanted to find a way to help grow others. I enjoyed speaking and training to help people succeed in their business, and I wanted to start my own business. I've been a fan of John Maxwell since I began reading personal development. I found his approach to leadership very easy to grasp, and I could apply his principles to my life and work almost immediately. Through his books, podcasts, and email newsletters, I found he had a certification program to become a speaker, trainer, teacher, and coach of his material. It seemed like a great opportunity for me to have a foundation to build on for a business, so I joined the John Maxwell Team in the spring of 2016 and started my business, J3 Motivation. I started mastermind groups and lunch-and-learns around my busy schedule and facilitated a few training sessions for companies. Most of the topics I would teach were about leadership. The Utah Black Chamber was gaining a lot of momentum, and I used the relationships that I had in the chamber community as a base to start my business. I began with just friends and community members and then began having success bringing on local companies as clients. A few organizations invited me to be their keynote speaker. Because the chamber was showing success and people had seen me lead chamber events, people were more accepting to attend a mastermind or a lunch-n-learn than trying to recruit them into a network marketing business. Training on personal growth without trying to sell a product or an opportunity behind it was a lot easier for me. And as the chamber continued to grow, I didn't worry about having any imposter syndrome. I was able to share the results of the leadership principles I was teaching when I applied them to the work I was doing with the chamber. Business was good when I worked it, but the challenge was having a full-time job and a growing chamber thatI was leading. In the back of my head, I knew what I ultimately wanted to do. I wanted to have my own business. Now the next step was trying to figure out how to get the chamber in a position to have a new leader. I knew if I did that, business would get even better, not just because I have more time, but it would be an even larger testament to my training and teaching on leadership.

In 2018, the topic of diversity, equity, and inclusion was becoming more at the forefront of conversations in private and public entities. Utah's growth was accelerating; however, diverse talent was challenging to recruit and retain. I wasn't strong at teaching this topic, but as more and more calls came, I leaned on a few people to educate me and partner with me to seize those opportunities. I found training and speaking on this material natural for me to share because I was applying these principles while I was growing the chamber, and I was able to share my own experiences as a Black man growing up in Utah. The growth provided personal stories and examples to share that resonated with my audience. In 2020, civil unrest was at a peak after the murder of George Floyd, and my phone and email were busier than ever before. I was doing a lot more speaking on diversity, equity, and inclusion than I was on leadership. While I enjoyed those opportunities, it was not my focus as it may have appeared to others since I led a diverse business organization. My focus was on leadership and growing leaders. I continued down the path of whatever opportunities came to me to help build my name, though, hoping that over time, I'll be able to build a stronger brand for my business.

I enjoy showing people how they can grow personally. Providing a resource, an introduction, or sharing my experience and knowledge is a little addicting. Presenting in front of a room to an audience has always been my main vehicle for that, but then masterminds started to become my favorite type of meeting to host. A mastermind is just a small group of 8-10 people who would meet every week and discuss a topic or a book. I would start off the topic and then facilitate the discussion. I loved hearing from the attendees about how this information could be applied to their life and impact their growth. There were sessions I rarely spoke at all and allowed the group to share. Every now and then, I would interject a question or respond to someone to get the group to think deeper. From here, I grew to really enjoy being a facilitator or moderator for discussions. I found that I could ask questions and keep a discussion going. Whenever I would be asked to speak at an event, I would try to modify the presentation to a panel discussion. Hearing different perspectives on a topic is a lot stronger than just one person presenting. Currently, I'll provide training and be a keynote for corporations, but at many of the community events I participate in, I'll put myself in as a facilitator to lead a discussion with other influencers.

EXPAND YOUR INFLUENCE THROUGH YOUR GIFTS

I believe passion is found through the talents and gifts you were given. They were given to you for a reason – for a purpose – to go out and live the life you were made to live. When you recognize what those gifts are and find your passion, your purpose is automatic. Once you commit to that purpose, the 'world will conspire to bring good to you.'

"Until one is committed, there is hesitancy, the chance to dwarf back, always ineffectiveness. Concerning all acts of initiative and creation, there is one elementary truth of the ignorance of which kills countless ideas and splendid plans; that the moment one commits oneself, providence moves too. All sorts of things occur to help one that would never otherwise have occurred. A whole stream of events issues from the decision, raising to one's favor all manner of unforeseen incidents and meetings and material assistance which no one could have dreamed would come her way. Whatever you can do or dream you can begin it. Boldness has genius, power, and magic in it."

– JOHANN WOLFGANG VON GOETHE

You cannot stop a person who is fully passionate and committed to their purpose. Throughout my journey, I have been so blessed to have the experiences and successes because I was passionate. Any time I had a doubt, I struggled. But when I fully committed to what I wanted to accomplish, somehow, a way was made. Throughout the rest of this book, you will learn about my journey to becoming a person of influence and how that played a whole in living my purpose. You cannot live with purpose without growing your influence. Your purpose is going to take more than just you. You'll need resources and people to support you in your growth and strategy. The African Proverb says, "If you want to go fast, go alone. If you want to go far, go together." Just like it takes a village to raise a child, it will take a village for you to live out your purpose.

REFLECTION

John Maxwell says that "Leadership is influence. Nothing more, nothing less." Once I understood that simple definition, my leadership began to grow, and as my leadership grew, so did my influence. Who do you currently influence beyond your family? Who do you influence that could support your purpose?

5

ENDURANCE: THE PROCESS

"Freedom is not lost when you are enslaved by chains to your ankles or wrists. Freedom is actually gained when you hold fast and strong to the chains that bind your faith. In other words, you can be restrained by your situation, yet still find joy knowing you're just in the process."

– DARNELL SELF

HOW MANY TIMES have you gotten excited about something, started on it, but never finished? The end result seemed awesome at the time, but as you started to dive into it, you quickly became discouraged by challenges or barriers that arose. Going into it, you knew it wasn't going to be easy, and even though you thought you would be able to endure, your desire to keep going waned and died. How do you stay committed to the end?

I love to hike. Utah's landscape provides amazing hiking opportunities all around the state. We have five national parks, several canyons, and amazing mountain ranges within our 'backyard.' From my current home, two canyons are just at the top of my neighborhood. There are small hikes, a couple of miles or less, or for those up for the challenge, hikes that can go over a dozen miles. The end of these hikes will have an arch, a body of water, a rock formation, or an amazing view of the world we live in. Depending on the length of the hike, it requires certain preparation – hiking boots and proper attire, a backpack, plenty of water, and an understanding of the trail, either a trail app, map, or saved image so you know where you are going. Most importantly, you have to be physically prepared for your adventure. A hike can require a certain amount of endurance, depending on the level. You may have a steep incline; you may need to climb over rocks, walk through water, navigate through a slot canyon, or even a little climbing off a wall.

In many cases, the most challenging hikes will usually reward you with the most stunning view at the end. Whenever I plan a hike, I look at an app, review the grade levels of easy, moderate, or hard, read the reviews, view pictures, then make a decision on where I'd like to go. I go on the hike because I know what the end will be. Sometimes there may be some cool views or landscapes along the way, but I look forward to the end. During the hike, I also enjoy the company I have. We have conversations and support one another along the way, which makes the hike more pleasurable. Hikes can also be a great workout; those are the ones I enjoy the most. I like the exercise. I like the adventure. I prepare myself to go through whatever it takes to finish that hike. So, how can you bring that same attitude to life?

Even once you strive to live with purpose in your life, it doesn't mean that life still won't bring challenges. Growing is a process. You will still have the hills and rocks that life gives you to climb. You're learning new things about life and yourself. What you have to ask yourself is, do you want challenges to promote you or defeat you? When you are living a life of no passion, defeat is always around the corner as you work simply just to get by. You'll often get discouraged and lack confidence in yourself. Dreams just seem like, well, – a dream, and you constantly find yourself "uncomfortably comfortable" in survival mode. Conversely, when you appreciate and embrace the process, you understand survival mode is part of the journey. It's to test you, teach you, and train you for the next level of your life. If embraced, life challenges are an investment into your future success.

When you have passion and live a life of purpose, you respond to challenges differently. You realize that everything happens in your life for a reason. Whether it be a lesson or blessing, it's important that you appreciate them both, knowing you're just in the process.

"TRUST THE PROCESS"

What is meant by "the process"? You may have some familiarity with this phrase. Simply put, it means embracing the challenges along the way to a promising outcome. The phrase became popular in 2013 by the NBA basketball team, the Philadelphia 76ers. The team acquired a new general manager, Sam Hinkie, to help turn around a team that had been struggling over the last few years. In his first speech with the team, he advocated an emphasis on a "process" over current outcomes. He knew his strategy of turning his team around would take some time, so he wanted everyone to anticipate struggles for a few years. Not everyone was a fan of this plan, including staff, some players, and of course, the fans. One of the people he won over, though, was one critical leader, head coach Brett Brown. Hinkie began trading away star players to get future draft picks to "rebuild the team."' During these trying times, the team fell to last place or close to last in the entire league. The following year, sportswriter Matt Lombardo tweeted, "Embrace the struggles for the rest of the year and trust in Hinkie, the process."

In 2014, Hinkie used one of those draft picks to acquire center Joel Embiid, an international and college star from the University of Kansas. However, due to injuries, he wasn't able to play until 2016. Embiid knew what he was capable of. He believed in the plan and believed he was the beginning of the Sixers' future success. He encouraged fans to *trust the process*, and as a result, he received the nickname "The Process." Before Embiid made an appearance on the court, the Sixers had a record-breaking losing streak in 2015, and Hinkie eventually resigned. Did that mean "the process" failed? Someone who initiated it all left the journey and would leave us to imagine he felt his plan failed and gave up. Well, in 2017, four years after the process began and the first full season Embiid was able to play on the court, the team finished in third place in the eastern conference and went to the playoffs. Since then, they have remained a competitive team and have made the playoffs nearly every year since.

Trust the Process has spread beyond the Philadelphia 76ers and its fans into a culture at large. The phrase has been used for inspiration, to remind people that "things may not be great right now, but have faith they'll work out." Have you set a goal, only to experience barriers, obstacles, or challenges that discouraged you from pressing forward? Did you overcome it? How did you gain trust in yourself or the process to keep moving? If you didn't press forward, what was the breaking point for you? Looking back, what could you have done differently to keep moving? Many authors and speakers have coined their own phrases of the process. One of the books that stuck out to me about the process was a book by sales trainer, Jeff Olson, called *The Slight Edge*. In this book, Olson shares how doing the simple things consistently over a period of time will put you on the path to achieve goals. For example, what if you wanted to read ten books in a year because you know that may be one of the things required to help you grow to become the person to achieve the goals you set? Break that down. How many pages is that a day? Would that require just ten pages? Ten books seem like a lot of reading, but ten pages may seem like a better goal you can commit to every single day. What if you wanted to lose 20 pounds? I was taught that you have to burn over 1,500 calories to lose one pound. So how many calories must you burn to lose 20 pounds? A lot! But what if you committed to eating healthy and burning 500 calories a day for two months? Does that seem more realistic?

Jeff Olson's *Slight Edge* teaches the philosophy of focusing and committing to the little things consistently over a period of time to reach what you desire. What if it could become something as little as changing your thought process? Many of us have heard this quote: "Thoughts become words, words become actions, actions become habits, habits become character, character becomes your destiny." This reminds us that just committing to an action like changing your thoughts can lead to changing the whole outcome of your life.

MILO OF CROTON

Milo was a 6th-century BC wrestler who won several Olympic events, even past a normal athlete's prime. Historians believe he was over 40 when he competed in his last Olympiad. The story goes that when he was a boy, he gained immense strength by lifting a newborn calf and carrying it on his shoulders. Legend has it that he returned the next day and carried out the same feat. Milo continued to do this for four years, hoisting the calf onto his shoulders each day as it grew until he was no longer a calf but a 4-year-old bull. Can you imagine picking up a bull over your shoulders? When it's a bull, it seems impossible. However, if you start picking up the calf over your shoulders every single day when you're young and continue as you grow and the calf grows into a bull for four years, could it be possible? The calf becomes lighter as you become stronger. But you can't take the shortcut. You have to be willing to commit to the process every single day, and eventually, you may be able to take the 4-year-old bull over your shoulders. The message of this story is to remind you to stay committed and patient and allow the journey to take hold. You may have challenging days or days that you just don't want to, but if you desire to have that end goal and are passionate about your purpose, no matter the circumstances, you'll get up and pick that bull over your shoulders.

MY PROCESS

I took advantage of many opportunities to identify the right vehicle for me to live out my purpose. I probably stayed in the network marketing company a lot longer than I should have, but it taught me so much about myself. I learned resilience and perseverance. Even when business was hard, and we weren't producing much, I stayed focused. I worked with our team and our leaders. I read books that could elevate my leadership and mindset. It was there that I learned "the process" and worked to stick to my commitments to the end–identifying if I am on the right path in identifying what I am passionate about and truly living my purpose. Leaving the network marketing business was difficult for me, even when I was losing more money than making money. I didn't want to fail. I was taught that failure wasn't an option. However, I believe if you are not living your purpose, failure is part of the process of growth. Recognizing this was the wrong vehicle took a while for me to admit and be okay with it. But once I did, I felt a huge weight lifted off my shoulders and then began to wonder why it was so hard to leave in the first place. Having a side hustle for almost a decade of my life, the part of life where I was learning adulthood, did set an expectation for me going forward. I was already in the process of learning how to start a Black chamber for the state of Utah. While it wasn't necessarily a '"hustle," it did fill a need for me. I was fine taking a break from a part-time income opportunity. That pressure was too much for me at this point, and I got more focused on my budget and worked on getting myself back into a comfortable financial position.

Where I was at that point, my life wasn't comfortable for me. It was hard to hang out with some friends as I compared myself to them. They all seemed to be doing better than me, and I felt I was working a lot harder than they were. It was easy for me to get discouraged that I wasn't living the lifestyle I thought I should be by then. I kept thinking that I shouldn't have even entered the network marketing business, and then I began to wonder about other choices I made that put me in the position I was in at that time. Was I in the right job? Did I really want to be in the finance industry? Theodore Roosevelt said, "Comparison is the thief of joy." I kept reminding myself of that and tried to be inspired or encouraged by them rather than comparing myself to them. We all take different paths in this life. There is no cookie-cutter" process for everyone. Those that believe there is one are usually not living their best life. I learned to be grateful for the people that surrounded me. Much of how you are is determined by your influences, the people you hang around the most, and my circle began to shift, introducing me to a new environment, and I seemed to be finding a new path for me.

It took time for me to not only believe the path I began to take, but also believe that I was worthy of taking this trek. Believing in myself was the most important piece of living with purpose. Joel Embiid knew he was the answer to the team's challenges, and he was willing to take on the mission of getting the team to be championship-worthy. It's your passion that will keep you going through all the challenges that you will inevitably encounter. Your passion will push you through the process to victory.

REFLECTION

Going through a process is a test of strength and endurance. It's a test of your passion for the mission you are embarking on. When entering this mission, really consider if the process is worth it. Your purpose should always be bigger than yourself, and when you are working for something beyond yourself, you'll find your commitment will also rise. What part of the process are you in right now in living your purpose? What are you struggling with, and what do you need to do to overcome those challenges?

PART TWO
THE WONDER YEARS

6
PASSION: WAYMON TISDALE III

"*I believe in destiny. But I also believe that you can't just sit back and let destiny happen. A lot of times, an opportunity might fall into your lap, but you have to be ready for that opportunity. You can't sit there waiting on it. A lot of times you are going to have to get out there and make it happen.*"

– SPIKE LEE

THE 1990S WERE the most memorable time of my life. Many people would say that their 20s or even 30s were the turning point in their lives. For me, those were just the second and third decades of my life. You may ask why I feel that the moments that happened in my life from 10 to 20 defined me. I didn't realize it was my turning point at the time, but all of my achievements and success, and all that I will accomplish, I can attribute to my experiences during that time. I didn't even realize it until I began writing this book. I thought that I loved the 90s because it had the best music (it's all been downhill from there), but it meant so much more to me than that.

In 1991, R&B music mogul, Andre Harrell, produced the film *Strictly Business*. Harrell created the record companies that elevated hip hop and R&B to new heights when he formed Uptown Records after spending time with Russell Simmons at Def Jam. Harrell is also known for discovering music legends Sean "P. Diddy" Combs and Mary J. Blige. In addition to music, he went on to produce movies. *Strictly Business* may not have been an Oscar winner or even much of a memorable film for most. It only grossed about $8 million. My view is that it was made for a targeted audience, and I was part of that audience. The plot was so relatable to me.

Joseph C. Phillips plays the character Waymon Tisdale, III, who is about to become the only Black partner at a commercial real estate firm. Waymon has a friend, Bobby (played by Tommy Davidson), who works as a low-level mail clerk at the same firm and helps him meet the girl of his dreams, Natalie, played by "my celebrity girlfriend," Halle Berry. I admit, it was Halle Berry that made me want to watch the movie in the first place. And I was an immediate fan of Waymon Tisdale III. Waymon was me. Not because he liked Natalie like I did, but because he had the same challenges of being Black as I did.

Growing up Black in Utah was hard. It was extra challenging being shy and introverted as well. My response to racism, bully-ing, or any other fascinating experiences about my Blackness was just to shut down or ignore it, pretending I didn't hear so I didn't have to deal with it. Even though that didn't make it any easier, the alternative was too hard for me to do. My comfort was in my family and my church. My family knew who I was, and I could be my goofy fun self. At church, I didn't have to worry about being Black. I got to learn about being Black. However, sometimes I worry about "being Black enough."

Waymon didn't care about "fitting in" until he saw Natalie for the first time. He was fine being the person he was. Waymon was successful and moving up in the world. In the beginning of the movie, Waymon is annoyed by Bobby. He didn't see Bobby really going anywhere in life, but at the same time, he was a little envious of Bobby being able to fit into the Black culture. Waymon didn't speak the slang, know all the "good music, the dance moves, or even how to speak to a woman like Natalie. He just wasn't familiar with the 'hip hop' culture.

As much as I was familiar with hip-hop culture, I was often too shy to put it on display outside of my family. African-Americans learn the ability to "code switch." Code-switching is when we adjust our language to fit into a dominant culture. My whole life was all about trying to fit in. My main goal was to perform well in school, get good grades, and go to college, so I could go out and land a great career similar to Waymon's. But I wanted both. Waymon wanted both. Waymon wanted both because he wanted to call Natalie his girlfriend. I wanted both because I just didn't want my Blackness to be questioned while on my path of being successful. We all have our identity crises when we're teenagers. I felt mine was at an extreme level because I just didn't know how James Jackson III fit into anything. I tried sports, music, and even acting in a play. At least Waymon had the confidence to even try to meet Natalie. I didn't talk to any girl unless I knew it was guaranteed the feeling was mutual, and even after that point, I still struggled.

At the end of most movies, the guy gets his dream. I'm sorry to spoil it here for you if you haven't seen this movie or have any desire to watch it, but Waymon gets Natalie as his girl, becomes a partner in his firm, and becomes comfortable with who he is as a person. It wasn't about being Black enough. It was about recognizing who he was as a person and that was Black enough for him, for Natalie, and for Bobby. As cliche as it may sound, I, too, have the same ending. I got my girl, found my passion, and am now living with a purpose, using my potential with an understanding of who I am and what I am capable of.

I'M ALL STRICTLY BUSINESS

I worked for twelve years at my first job, Morgan Stanley. I started right out of college. I began in the collections department, which was way out of my comfort zone. Calling people to collect on their late bills was not fun for me. I was terrible at it in the beginning, but over time, I grew some confidence and found my way to grow in the department. Call center jobs were the best-paying entry-level jobs for the path I wanted to grow into at the time, so I endured the journey knowing a great outcome would come at the end. From collections, I moved to customer service and began managing projects and teams. One project, in particular, was helping to rebuild our customer management system, and the company sent me to New York to meet with executives and developers. I loved the New York trips. They were quick trips, but it was New York! And because it was such a long flight, I got to fly in a day early and leave a day later, so I had more time to explore than my other colleagues who worked out east. Their flights were a lot shorter, so they were able to arrive the day the meetings started and leave the same day the meetings ended. Once the trips stopped and it was the "normal grind" again, I realized the opportunities to move around were limited for what I wanted to do.

In 2009, seven years into my career at Morgan Stanley, I met Michelle. She was happily single with three children, and I was six months divorced, trying to find myself again. I never expected to fall in love again so soon, but she got my heart quickly with her drive, personality, and beauty. I met her children one year later. Zoe, Memphis, and Audrie are amazing. They, as well as myself, are so fortunate to have Michelle's influence in our lives. Three years later, we all moved in together. Michelle began to see the grind. The last year was getting hard, but I didn't know exactly where else I wanted to go. The benefits somewhat handcuffed me to the company. What other company was going to provide what they offered at that age in my field? Did I want to stay in this field? I grew up loving numbers, so I thought finance was the route for me. I was hoping that network marketing was my way out, but I was beginning to fizzle out there as well. I think both the struggle of network marketing and reaching my end point of the company, Michelle saw my pain in the morning as I got up early to be in the office by 7 AM. I felt like I was at a dead end.

After work one day, she sat down with me and shared that she saw my anguish and suggested that it was time to leave Morgan Stanley. She mentioned that there could be an opportunity to pair as a team with her originating residential mortgage loans, which would give me a lot more freedom, offer more rewarding work, and potentially be more fun. I thought long and hard about this option. Even though I no longer enjoyed what I was doing, change is hard, especially if you have been at the same company for over a decade. And not just going to another job but a different industry where I would have to learn new skills.

It took a couple of weeks before I agreed to make the shift. Sometimes we get comfortable being uncomfortable. Even though we don't like it, it's familiar, and we know how to navigate. Stepping into a new environment that is unfamiliar is tough. Since we don't know how to navigate or what to expect, it is a different type of discomfort. Even when we don't like it, just knowing the expectations keeps us trapped. This is why change is hard. This is why people stay in unhealthy relationships. They know it's not good for them, even when their life is on the line, but they stay there because they know how to manage it. Some will try something new with the same mindset, and they fail, so they revert back to their old ways.

If you haven't found your passion, you must consider change. Staying in the same mindset, in the same environment, and even the same influence can block you from realizing the purpose of why you're here – the reason you have been equipped with the gifts and talents. You're now just going through experiences to prepare you for your purpose. At the beginning of working in the mortgage business, it was fun. I was enjoying this new world and learning new things. Not being tied to a desk all the time was what I found to love the most. I enjoyed making new connections while learning new skills in a new industry. I was going to golf tournaments with clients, attending social events, and doing community projects. Michelle was a top producer, and she was invited to attend a trip with other top producers at a five-star resort in Laguna Beach. Traveling was one of our favorite things to do, and that was an amazing trip. We also attended a summit in Sunriver, Oregon. This conference was for mortgage and real estate professionals and taught us business and life planning. I wasn't clocking in and out, watching my hours and break times. I was working with people with an entirely different lifestyle than those working in a call center. Could this be the move for me? I thought so at first. That was the fun side, though. The mortgage industry was not easy for me. Even though this was during the time of low-interest rates and housing was a lot more affordable, getting my mortgage license, learning the process and systems, compliance and legal requirements, and connecting with real estate agents was challenging for me. I was so used to a structured day and I had to learn how to build and manage my own schedule.

Working with your life partner is not easy either. Some couples can do it, but it's not for everyone, and that's okay. Over time, it was challenging for Michelle and me to work together. We had different mindsets on how to work. Michelle was more organized and had a very effective system. My role was to support her in those systems and do a lot of the relationship-building with real estate agents, which was not one of her favorite things to do. In the beginning, I was excited about it, but it came down to bringing business in and closing deals. That wasn't happening enough compared to my activity. The lack of production from me began impacting my confidence. This was a similar feeling I had in networking marketing. Here we go again, I feared. Michelle began seeing a different James than the one she met. I was struggling with my confidence and began questioning who I was and who I wanted to be. I was getting tired of failing at things, and now I was failing here with my partner. We worked together for only a couple of years before I left that role and started another chapter.

The Black Chamber was gaining some momentum, and we had developed a great relationship with the regional bank, Zions Bank. Zions Bank was the first company to support the chamber. They had a role I felt I would be great for. It was in the diverse markets department serving as a banker for diverse local businesses. I had been familiar with this team for several years and became great friends with the bankers. The role was similar to what I was doing at the mortgage company, but working with small businesses was more up my alley, especially diverse ones. And since I led the Black Chamber and had strong connections to the other minority ethnic chambers, I felt this would be a great position for me. I recall wondering why I never considered applying for this position in the first place. But timing is everything. Where I was now in leadership, in the chamber, and community, I was more qualified than when I was first introduced to the team. I asked for a position and it didn't take long for them to consider me a good fit. Having never been in banking before, however, I was drinking from a fire hose most of the time. It didn't bother me, though. I was excited about this new role and working with friends and in a community that I was already working with. Many bankers took me under their wing, mentored me, and helped close deals. The events we attended were events I usually attend or try to attend, but now I have a bank supporting my attendance, and I served a different purpose.

One of the greatest things about this experience is that I was already in this environment with the Black Chamber. I worked with the team before, so I was familiar with expectations. The combination of working for the bank and leading the chamber helped me realize my passion. I liked having a "quiver of arrows" to use to solve problems in the community, not just for the small businesses, but having a company with other services to support them. To this day, I feel more like an ambassador for Zions Bank than an employee. All employers should strive for their employees to feel this way. It's the main reason why I haven't left the institution. What I do there continues to serve my purpose. Even though I have worked in different roles since I started, they always tie back to my purpose. In my most recent role, I had the honor of designing and implementing the company's supplier diversity program. The purpose of this program is to increase our spend with diverse businesses in our supply chain strategy. Providing opportunities for diverse businesses with a large regional bank? The role couldn't be more perfect while I continue to grow the Black Chamber. The sense of security of having a job has been nice as well. Many would want to strive to become independent and have their own business, which would be my goal eventually, but as long as you're passionate about something and your job supports your passion, what's the rush to leave?

WHAT DID I WANT TO BE WHEN I GREW UP?

Most of us are not in the career we dreamed of growing up. When I was young, I was never confident in knowing what I wanted to be when I grew up. I felt obligated that I had to choose something, though. I began with the dream of being a professional athlete, but my small size made that a challenge for basketball and football. I should have learned to play soccer or run track! Then I thought physical therapy or sports medicine would be a good route for me, but I just didn't do well in any science classes, so I disqualified that route. Same thing with being an engineer. I was good at math, but when I found that some science would be part of the path, I stopped. What was I passionate about? Some find their passion when they're young and live out their dream. Some never find their passion and live a life of mediocrity. But it doesn't have to be both extremes for you. If you haven't found your passion, it's never too late. Once you find your passion, you will find the light for your life. Light provides vision, and you're able to see further down your path. Light provides a new perspective. Have you ever walked into one of the rooms in your house thinking it looks the same way you left it, but when you turn it on, something has changed, or you notice something different? Passion is the light.

From these career experiences, I realized over time that there is a difference between commitment and passion. My "loyalty complex" was just commitment. It was hard to leave something, especially when I felt I hadn't achieved what I wanted out of that position. I had agreed to a responsibility and wanted to stick to it. Commitment is an obligation. Passion is a strong desire. Commitment is action. Passion is an emotion. Commitment keeps us coming back. Passion gets us talking about the need for change. Commitment is applauded. Passion is contagious. For success, the two must go hand in hand. However, you can have commitment but have no passion, like the first job I had. But if you're passionate, commitment automatically follows. The jobs that I left, I was committed to them, but I wasn't passionate about them. Nothing was inspiring me to thrive. I was committed to being great, but greatness won't show up if you're not passionate. And if you're passionate, the commitment is when you show up early to an event to not only set up but to visualize what it could be, and stay late after to not only clean up, but think about how to make it better next time. That was my process at all the chamber events. I was always the first one there and the last one to leave. Commitment is doing something you have never done before with confidence and enthusiasm because you know the impact it will bring. Passion is coming out of your own pocket when funds are low because you have so much faith in the process.

It was my passion to make an impact and the endurance to carry through. I'm passionate about sharing my journey to bring more impact. I want to share how you can grow your influence. Your influence, no matter your desired path, will bring you more success. And the biggest battle is your endurance to push through, no matter the challenge. My hope for you after reading this book is that you will begin to live a life of passion, influence, and endurance, giving you the ability to live the life you imagined it to be. I may not have imagined this life watching Waymon Tisdale find his path to having the girl of his dreams would inspire me to find my path to having the life of my dreams, but it showed me that if you're passionate enough, you have the right ability to influence, and have the endurance to achieve your goal, no matter how long or how it takes, your "Natalie" is within your reach.

REFLECTION

Many of us are not in the career we desired as kids. Life circumstances or just growing up took us on a different path. Are you happy with your current career path? If so, how come? If not, what will it take for you to change course? Whether it is finding your passion or finding the willingness to change, don't wait too long. I've learned there's never a right time. The best time is always now. If you decide to wait, you could end up waiting your whole life.

7

INFLUENCE: GROWING MY LEADERSHIP

"We will all, at some point, encounter hurdles to gaining access and entry, moving up and conquering self-doubt, but on the other side is the capacity to own opportunity and tell the story."

– STACEY ABRAMS

WHILE NETWORK MARKETING taught me a lot about leadership, I was still very raw and new to leadership. I was also still new to being full-time in the workforce when I started just after graduating college. It was the first time that people depended on my leadership as part of their overall growth and success. The pressure to help them succeed, however, didn't affect me as much as wanting to become the person who could help them succeed. I was reading books and trying to apply the concepts I was learning, but there were other elements of my growth that needed work, like my own confidence and being the example I wanted to be.

JEKYLL & HYDE

I also felt like I was living two separate lives. At work, I was taking customer service calls and supporting financial advisors. I worked just hard enough so they wouldn't fire me, not really seeking to move up because I was convinced that what I was doing part-time in network marketing was eventually going to replace this job. In the evening, I was focused on changing the lives of others, doing sales presentations and calls. I was a completely different person. Over time, though, I realized this mindset wasn't working. My personal growth felt like it hit its peak, which was stunting the growth of the business. After learning more about leadership from reading more books and attending conferences, I realized that I needed to be my whole self everywhere, all the time. Not operating at a consistent level of striving to maximize my potential was impacting my overall potential. Different environments provide different opportunities to help you grow, and it's important you take advantage of all of those opportunities. Whether it's a job you work at, a community service project, or raising a family, you put different skills and abilities to the test which help you to grow.

There was one manager, Kazua, that saw the same potential in me like Michael did when he sought me to take over the Black Chamber. I wasn't the only one who was drawn to her leadership. Many service representatives desired to be on her team. It was the way she connected with her employees. Kazua had a nurturing way of leading and led with integrity. She always had faith in all her employees, even those with the worst performance. She identified their strengths and helped them build from them. For me, she saw that I could perform better than I was. When we had our one-on-one meetings, it was easy for me to talk to her. Our meetings always ran over time. She knew how to encourage me to elevate my performance. After a couple of years of being on her team, I was one of her top representatives, and she leaned on me to support the team with any challenges in handling their calls. She gave me special projects to work on, and I was spending less time on the phone.

About a year later, Kazua approached me about applying for a manager position. I wasn't sure I was ready, and it took a few conversations before she convinced me to apply. There were already discussions from upper management about me moving up. The role was mine to lose. Once I was in that role, I didn't know what I was so worried about. I had developed the competitive nature inside of me, and I wanted to have the best team on the entire floor. I took some tips from being on her team and refined them into my personality. Unbeknownst to me, many of the leadership concepts that I was using in my networking marketing business I was applying to work. It took a few months, but when I found my leadership style, my team was one of the top-performing teams.

Upper-level management appreciated my knowledge of the systems and how I led as well. They invited me to more special projects in addition to managing my team. One of the projects was assisting in designing the overall service platform the employees used to service customers and financial advisors. My role was as one of the subject matter experts (SME), where I provided a scope of how the representatives serviced the calls they received and what was needed for them to be more efficient. We met with developers in New York a few times, and of all the business trips I have taken over the course of my career, as you know, those were my favorite. We didn't have long meetings like a conference or summit or meeting with different associates throughout the day. We just had one big long meeting, and we all hung out afterward for dinner and drinks. I had time to experience New York and connect with the developers and my other teammates in person.

I felt this was the moment when I transitioned from this shy but motivated person into a hungry and ambitious young leader. I was becoming more comfortable with myself. Being introduced to a greater potential when one moves towards becoming a person of influence inspired me to focus not so much on the opportunities that I currently had or what they could be but more on what I could become and what would happen if I focused more on developing myself. Author and business leader, Jim Rohn, said, "Work harder on yourself than you do at your job. If you work hard on your job, you'll make a living. If you work hard on yourself, you'll make a fortune." I was more willing to make changes when necessary if it involved growing my leadership. If I wasn't in this mindset, I don't know if I would have been willing to move on from Morgan Stanley and work with Michelle in mortgages. I've always had a hard time moving on from things that I have grown used to. Routine is part of my nature. Even when it's not going well or is not good for me, it's hard to change away from it because it's a system to me that I have grown accustomed to. Michelle often encouraged me to try new things, food, the outdoors, and other recreational activities. Now that I have expanded my ability to make changes within, it's given me more opportunities to grow. John Maxwell teaches that in life, breakthroughs occur in people and organizations when they hurt enough, and they have to change, learn enough so that they want to change or receive enough that they can change.

A NEW FOCUS

Working in mortgages with Michelle wasn't as successful as we both planned, and it really tested my ability for me to change and adapt. This time of my life felt like a failure to me, but I learned a lot about myself, and when I stepped into the new role at Zions Bank, I came in with excitement and confidence. I fully let go of things holding me down, such as the network marketing business, understanding this was all part of "the process" for me, and I would begin to trust God more along with the process."

This transition also allowed me to focus more on the Black Chamber. With more focus came more support, and with more support came more growth. The growth provided a bigger vision of what could be for this organization. With this 'new me,' I began to see my overall influence in the community grow. Between the role I had at the bank and the role I played in the chamber, I was everywhere in the community: galas, business expos, networking social, you name it. I attended every community event at least once! I began to learn Utah's strength in community and collaboration. There were organizations that had a large platform that were easy to connect with and influencers the same. Resources for small businesses became more visible, and I identified key individuals to connect with and established a relationship. Internally, I learned the strategy of how the bank maintained itself as a community influencer. A few years into my career, I moved to its community development department. I saw the sponsorship requests that came in, and I followed a few to see the outcome of those requests. That helped me understand how to build sponsorship requests for the chamber. Zions has always been a big supporter of the chamber, but I was able to gain several other strong supporters and began to establish a firm foundation for the organization. It allowed me to implement systems for better efficiency which gave me more capacity to identify more board members and leaders to expand the vision.

S.Y.S.T.E.M

To maintain the chamber's growth, my growth at the bank, and my sanity, I needed to develop a process to help me become more efficient. I am a very routine-based person, and processes and systems help me stay organized and on task. I learned that system was an acronym, Save YourSelf Time, Energy, and Money. An effective system helps you become more efficient with your time. A system can be a combination of resources, software applications, establishing a team, or a daily calendar you can commit to. When you have a day that's planned out, and it's able to be maintained, you are more prepared with the right energy and understanding. When you don't plan your day, you tend to expend more energy and sometimes even more money than you would like. For example, who is more likely to spend less money – the employee who brings lunch to work every day or the one who doesn't? One employee has the week planned out for lunch, while the other feels they have the budget to eat out every day, but the lunch varies depending on where you are going and who you are going with. Also, the employee who brings lunch would typically eat lunch at their desk, the breakroom, or someone close to the office, allowing them to get back to work in a timely manner. If you're eating out, you're likely spending more time traveling and waiting for your food. If I don't have a system in place, I found myself just tackling whatever I could whenever and however I could. I was like an octopus on roller skates; I had a bunch of activity but not a lot of direction. A system helps put me on a path forward.

I got the chamber a CRM, a customer relationship management system, and a new website, so members can join online, and we can track membership and provide more value to our members. Once we added this system, we began to experience exponential growth. New board members came with new energy to volunteer and help with guidance and events. The small business resources in the community had programming and training that supported our members, so we established partnerships and referred our members to them rather than working to develop our own programming. Any type of programming the chamber had was mainly focused on introducing members to the community and resources and vice versa. We simply maintained ourselves as a hub and a bridge. An effective system in place allowed me to focus more on establishing the relationships I needed and work to become a stronger person of influence in the community. I discovered other ethnic minority chambers of commerce in addition to the Hispanic Chamber, more diverse business organizations, resources, and partners that could support the growing vision of the Utah Black Chamber.

IT HAS TO BE A WIN-WIN

The strongest partnerships I developed came when each of us had mutual interest or value from the relationship. These are the types of relationships I maintain today. Coming from a servant-leader mindset, I am focused on the value I bring to the relationship. It can't just be about the products or services the bank provides or what value the chamber gains from someone joining. The value has to go both ways. I don't have it in me just to take all the time. Even when it is offered or if deserved, either indirectly or down the road later, there's reciprocation in some form. If a member joins the chamber, I want to be sure they are receiving the benefits that we promised to them. If a corporation joins the chamber, I meet with them to discuss what they are seeking out of their membership. I look at them more as a partner than just a member. They have resources and an influence that can support the small businesses and the chamber, and we have a connection to the community they wouldn't have if they weren't connected to us. Even as a banker, if I am working with the client, I know we have the products and services they need for their business, but I want that business to grow, so I look to other resources the bank has internally or other partners that could support them. Whenever I meet with a Black business about banking products, it is a win-win-win, because, between the chamber and the bank, I have a quiver of resources to share with them.

"The more responsibility you take, the more control you have of your destiny."

OWNING IT

I was frustrated with the local leadership within the networking marketing company. Our region became less and less welcoming and it was becoming less desirable to engage. It was one of the reasons the decision to walk away was easier for me. Once the New York trips at Morgan Stanley stopped, I felt there were no more opportunities left for me there. The trips had opened me up to what opportunities the company had and what I desired. Utah doesn't have a lot of diversity, so it's tough to grow an organization whose focus is on the smallest diverse community. Yet, all of these statements were excuses planted in my head. The last one came from others and, in the beginning, gave me doubt if I would succeed. I began to grow tired of the excuses. We are often fed more negative thoughts by this world than positive ones. News, social media, and even family and friends can be "Debbie Downers." This is why it's so important to have a circle of influence around you that can keep you inspired and encouraged. I decided that "if it was up to be, it was up to me." Whether I produced something good or made a mistake, I owned all of it. Mistakes helped me grow, and my production pushed me further. Acknowledging any wrongdoing helped me become stronger in my leadership. Owning success grew my confidence. Seeing failure as a learning opportunity increased my knowledge and understanding. Recognition was my opportunity to strengthen my platform. I'm sure I still make more mistakes and have more failures than any successes or accomplishments I have had, but I also believe I wouldn't have those successes without those failures. When you're hungry enough to achieve your destiny, you must be willing to own every circumstance to control and design your own path.

REFLECTION

I believe that leadership is the most important ability when it comes to living with purpose. How do you rank your level of leadership? What opportunities do you have in your life that offer a path to grow your influence? Even if you don't seek leadership in your career, your family leans on your leadership. And if it is just you, it is even more important to become a leader of yourself. Don't allow others to control your circumstances. Own your destiny.

8

ENDURANCE: IT WAS ALL A DREAM

"I learned early on the magic of life is having a vision, having faith, and then going for it."

– ELAINE WELTEROTH

THE FALL of 2008 was a rough moment in my life. I failed in my first marriage and was moving back in with my parents. Living at home at 28 years old was not a good feeling. I appreciated being welcomed back and was grateful for the support, but I felt like a failure. Divorced, and living with my parents, I wasn't all that excited about my job at the time, and my network marketing business was beginning to wane. I was also trying to figure out how to start a Black Chamber and was struggling in that process. I'm pretty sure I was near depression. Then one night, I had a dream. I'm pretty sure this dream was the turning point from depression to obsession. It "woke me up" in every sense of the word. I felt this was one of God's ways of speaking to me.

THE DREAM

In the dream, I was on my way to a lunch meeting to give a networking marketing presentation. I was already running late, and as soon as I entered the freeway, I was stuck in traffic. I called and let my appointment know that I was running behind. While sitting in traffic, I began thinking about my life. *How can I start turning things around? There has to be something that will give me a spark. School came to my mind. Would I want to go back to school and get my master's degree? Where would I go, though? I don't want to take the GMAT. I think the University of Phoenix doesn't require the GMAT, and I can do all the courses online and wouldn't have to attend class in person. I think it's pretty affordable. How would I pay for it? Wait, I believe my company has tuition reimbursement. I'll look into that tomorrow.* After that thought, I found myself in the emergency lane but wasn't in my car anymore. I was on a bicycle, pushing it down the freeway with my feet instead of peddling. I don't know why I wasn't peddling, but I was still moving faster than all of the cars trying to move. Then as I look ahead, I see my exit in sight. That's when I woke up.

This is one of the few dreams that I remembered when I woke up. This is the only dream I remember so vividly. I took it as a message that I needed to take action. The next morning at work, I began researching the company benefits to find information about tuition reimbursement. After seeing what the benefits looked like, I started researching the University of Phoenix and its programs. Everything seemed to line up for me to go back to school, so I pulled the trigger that day, just hours after having that dream. I truly believed this was a spark I needed. There was no hesitation. No deeper thinking about it. Just action. I submitted the online application for their MBA program. Within a month, I was enrolled and began the first set of classes.

I thought more about the change of transportation from a car to a bicycle after I considered the idea of going back to school. Here I was, just pushing a bike down the emergency lane, but I was passing every car that was stuck in traffic. I was on my way to my exit faster than everyone else. Sometimes we may think we are in the wrong vehicle because it is out of the ordinary or it doesn't make sense to others. Going back to school later in life, trying to build a network marketing business, or starting a nonprofit to make an impact in the community may not be the traditional path to success. I once heard that we were not made to fit in. We are born to stand out. How often do you think of ideas, but choose not pursue them, because you begin to wonder what others would think or say about you? Have you ever wanted to pursue an opportunity but you didn't feel comfortable moving forward because it was so different from what you would normally pursue? It's one of life's dilemmas. We want change, but we don't want *to* change.

While in the program, everything began to get back on track for me. The classes provided the content to put me in the right direction. One of the classes I took was strategic planning, one of the lessons I needed to launch the Black Chamber. My leadership mindset changed, and I began working to move up the leadership ranks at work. I felt all of the negative energy around me begin to dissipate, and I felt my confidence coming back. That dream gave me a mindset shift and I knew everything was going to be alright. I received my master's degree two years later, in the spring of 2010. Life will throw challenges at you, but it's to help you become stronger so you can elevate your game. The only way to grow is to continue to rise above these barriers to get to the next level. From then on, I refused to allow life circumstances to get to me like this again by finding resources or other support to help me overcome them.

MICHELLE'S PASSION JOURNEY

As I was getting my head back on track and working to get back on my feet, I wasn't thinking about having another relationship for a while. However, life had other plans. A couple in my network marketing business invited me to one of their home meetings, and they wanted me to meet one of their friends, Michelle. Michelle was their mortgage lender, and they thought we would be good together. I thought they were so wrong. Michelle was similarly on the same page. She was not looking for a relationship either, and knowing that this meeting was a setup, she intentionally showed up way late. She was nice and attractive, but I didn't think I was ready for anything. I was not interested at first, but then we connected again after the meeting and here we are 14 years later still together. When you commit to a purpose, God, the universe, or whoever your higher power is, it will begin to commit along with you and provide you with opportunities and people to support you towards your purpose.

Michelle was the first hired employee of a local startup mortgage company. As the Executive Assistant and Assistant Mortgage Loan Consultant, her main role was assisting the owners, but she had her hand in everything. She trained and onboarded new staff, adding Onboarding Manager to her multiple roles. She was well-versed in all the systems to support her colleagues and loan officers. She enjoyed serving her customers. When she moved from assistant to a full-time mortgage loan consultant, I really got a chance to see her leadership skills. She said she hated sales, but her main skill was her service to her clients and her partners. Maya Angelou said, "People may remember not what you said or what you did, but they will always remember how you made them feel." Whenever her clients or partners talked to or about her, I thought about that quote. Michelle made them feel important, and she cared about them. It was more than just a transaction to her. It was a relationship. Because of that, she didn't have to do as much of the marketing and sales strategies that most loan officers do.

What really made Michelle beam, though, were community service projects. She loved serving the community. The company encouraged staff and salespeople to engage in the community. Because the company owners saw Michelle's passion for serving others, she was asked to lead these efforts. When she led the events, they were always well-organized and very well-attended. Even when I didn't work for the company, I partici-pated in the events and had a lot of fun. I found all the projects to be rewarding. She helped me understand how to serve the community. The first event that I remember participating in was raking leaves for the elderly. We visited different homes and cleaned up all the fall leaves from the yards of those who couldn't do so. It felt so good to help someone in need, and I gained many relationships through these events. Outside of her work role, Michelle joined some of her friends to support a back-pack drive. The company soon adopted that project and hosted backpack drives for an elementary school for several years. I'll never forget seeing the faces of the students receiving new back-packs full of school supplies before the first day of school. I couldn't imagine going to school with no supplies, and being able to provide for those students felt amazing. One of my favorite projects, though, was painting homes for the elderly, disabled, and veterans in the community. Michelle built a relationship with NeighborWorks Salt Lake, an organization that works to build and sustain housing and economic development in local neighborhoods. Each year, the organization seeks companies to sponsor and volunteer to help paint the homes of elderly residents. Consistently, Michelle recruited teams of volunteers from her company to paint houses. They brought their spouses and families to help paint as well. The labor was intense at times, but overall, it was a fun project. I enjoy painting. I am not a handyman by any means, but I am a good painter and enjoyed it. While it wasn't the main outcome Michelle was seeking, it also helped build and strengthen relationships with colleagues, partners, and potential clients as well. NeighborWorks Salt Lake presented Michelle with the Community Builder of the Year award in 2018. She continues to have a relationship to this day, and we look forward to painting houses every year.

Michelle always thought about leading her own nonprofit someday. She had a few ideas of what she wanted to do. She wanted to empower women. Michelle was a single mother of three children when I met her. She worked hard to provide for them and found her way into the mortgage business which provided her the opportunity to provide for her kids. She believes there's always a solution to every problem, and when given the chance and resources, people don't have to live with the challenges life gives them but use those challenges to strengthen and rise above. She wanted her story to empower other women. It wasn't hard to see what she was passionate about. However, until she found the right opportunity to push that passion towards her purpose, she used that passion to be successful in mortgage.

PUSHED BY PURPOSE

Michelle worked for that same company for 17 years, which is rare in the mortgage industry. Many loan officers will go from one company to another to find the best opportunity for them. That wasn't Michelle's MO. She was not only committed to her clients and partners, but she was also committed to the owners of the company, and mortgage was more of a vehicle for her than an opportunity. After 17 years, she decided this vehicle had come to a stop for her. The industry itself was changing, as well as some of the leadership around her. She also changed her outlook on things and wanted to find the right opportunity that was more meaningful. She took some time off to decide what her next opportunity was going to be. After about six months, Michelle joined her friend at another startup company in the real estate industry and kept her commitment to dedicate two years to helping build their processes and sales team. She knew she wasn't going to be there forever. While she had been at the mortgage company, she began volunteering for an organization focused on poverty alleviation, Circles Salt Lake. There were a few other chapters in Utah and this was a new one. She was introduced to this organization by a friend of hers and she was immediately sold on the mission. She really enjoyed the organization, and people saw her passion. After serving as a volunteer in many capacities for two years, she was asked to serve on the board and made an immediate impact. She made such an impact that she was asked to serve as board president. Coming from experience, starting a new nonprofit is challenging, and this one was no different. It took time to find the right leadership, build the board, and get volunteers. Within three years, they were on their second executive director, and in his third year, he announced that he would be leaving at the end of the year. Michelle thought this would be her chance to lead a nonprofit. She loved the purpose it served, and most of the individuals involved in the program were women. She had a strong relationship with many who were participating, as well as staff. When she hinted at the idea with the executive director and a few of the board members, they responded with enthusiasm that they were hoping she would put her name in the hat. After careful consideration, she officially applied for the position, and it wasn't long after she was hired as the new executive director for Circles Salt Lake by unanimous vote.

At first, the role was pretty daunting. There was a lot of work to be done, and not a lot of capacity or resources – the story of our lives in the nonprofit world! This was also a new organization still trying to become stable and needing more staff and volunteers. Now I may be biased since Michelle is my significant other, but in less than a year, Circles Salt Lake gained much more visibility and engagement in her first year as the Executive Director. She participated in other committees that aligned with Circles' mission. She found more supporters and volunteers to assist with programming and recruited a strong staff to support her. The flagship event of Circles programming is a weekly meeting with all circle leaders and allies. Community supporters provide dinner, and there is programming for the youth while the adults gather to discuss how to get out of poverty. Since Michelle took over, this meeting has consistently had someone donate meals, which had been a challenge before. Finding volunteers to help with the youth programming had also been a persistent challenge, but now, every week the youth are provided with a different activity, whether it's arts and crafts or learning something fun and new.

More volunteers and allies have come to Circles to engage, too. More and more, the community is recognizing Circles and its current and potential impact going forward. This all happened not just because of Michelle's leadership, but because of her passion. She was led by her passion, and people followed her because of her passion. People feel her energy and are moved by what she's working to accomplish. I get the inside scoop at home and feel her passion every single day. Through challenging times and good times, her commitment never wavers. When she's exhausted, or things are not working like she would like them to, she still gives it her all. When she's at her weekly meetings with program participants, staff, and volunteers, it is a whole new energy. I love seeing her in her role. I began to volunteer for her organization a few months ago. Michelle has supported me for the entire time I was leading the chamber. I feel it's not only fair that I reciprocate, but I am inspired by her work and I just get excited to see her in action. I am also excited to share any resource or relationship I have gained while building a nonprofit myself. Michelle has always been a great leader, but when you put passion behind it, your leadership can expand beyond your borders of influence.

Michelle has been a constant inspiration, encourager, and example for me. She has taught me so much about community service, leading the community, and connecting with people. I'm truly grateful for her and her passion. Often, we get told how much of a "power couple" we are. I agree, but I think we all know who holds the most power within this couple. Throughout this book, you'll read how much I have accomplished throughout the last 14 years, and Michelle has been there for all of it. She's seen the good, bad, and ugly and yet, she is still by my side. I was introduced to the kids, Zoe, Memphis, and Audrie, a year after we began dating, and I love them so much. I consider them my own, and they have grown to become wonderful human beings. The love and support from them and Michelle are the primary reasons I have been able to keep going.

REFLECTION

One of my mentors taught me that people come into our lives for a season or a reason. Everyone that enters your life has a purpose. Either they stay to provide, guide, or help you thrive, or they arrive to challenge, give perspective, and disappear. In either case, there are always opportunities to grow from experiences with relationships with people. What about the people in your life – family, friends, coworkers, or mentors? Have you considered their purpose for your life and how you can better cultivate that relationship? I have missed opportunities by not asking myself this question. In a society where relationships are as important or more important than capital, how much are you paying attention to the potential investment people in your life can pour into you?

PART THREE
UTAH BLACK CHAMBER

9

IN THE BEGINNING

"Go to work! Go to work in the morn of a new creation... until you have... reached the height of self-progress, and from that pinnacle bestow upon the world a civilization of your own.

– MARCUS GARVEY

NETWORKING WITH PURPOSE

Starting a nonprofit was never something I had any interest in doing. I had always wanted to engage in the community to make a meaningful impact, but what that looked like, I didn't know. Being a leader of a nonprofit or a leader of anything was always scary for me. Leading an organization in a network marketing company was comfortable for me because I didn't feel the pressure of a whole organization failing because of me. Everyone was operating independently, and my role was to motivate, inspire, and ensure my associates had me and other things as resources they needed to be successful. However, I was struggling to find success myself. I was quickly becoming part of the NFL, No Friends Left club, and I hated cold calling. I wanted to find other ways to find potential candidates, but not just anyone. I wanted real salespeople or professionals that would see this vision.

In trying different ways to connect to professionals, I discovered networking events. These events happened throughout my city and were hosted by different kinds of organizations. Some of these organizations were strictly networking organizations like BNI (Business Networking International), an individual or a group of individuals who host networking events to build their own network, or a company just trying to introduce themselves to the community. I attended many of these functions and failed miserably at my first networking attempts. I didn't know how to network. I didn't have the outgoing personality to just walk up to someone to strike up a conversation. Dajon was the better salesperson, so I played wingman for him mostly, and some-times even a hype man. When I felt things were going well, I just fed him more energy to keep talking to people. Over time though, as I observed his interactions with people and how others networked, I became a little more comfortable and found my way to talk to people. Sometimes, I would even attend events on my own. Soon, I was attending a networking event almost 3-4 times a month and started to become really good at it, building solid relationships and connecting well with people.

THE UTAH BLACK CHAMBER OF COMMERCE

From attending all these networking events, I discovered chambers of commerce. Cities throughout our county had their own chamber of commerce to support their local small businesses and community, and all of them hosted a monthly networking event for their members and welcomed non-members as well. I began to consistently crash their events, never intending to become a member of any of the chambers. I just wanted their network. Later, however, after founding my own chamber, I realized the value in becoming a member. People join a chamber to build their network, grow their businesses, and find opportunities to serve their community. In February 2006, leadership from our local Black community formed the Utah Black Chamber of Commerce. They held a press event introducing the chamber, its leadership, and its founding sponsors. I was excited about this because I knew there were many Black-owned businesses in the community that needed a chamber of commerce for support, and I could network within my own community with people who I am more comfortable with. What I wasn't prepared for, though, was that the chamber wasn't met with immediate success. The chamber events had very small numbers, and sometimes the events turned into planning sessions with the attendees to discuss how to grow the chamber better. "Where were all the people who attended the launch event?" I thought to myself. I was becoming a little disappointed in my community in its seeming lack of support for one another. Here was this potentially great resource, and it wasn't receiving the support that it expected. I had this urge to help, but I didn't know how.

After about a year, the chamber became quiet. Not many events were going on, and there was a growing concern about the organization not being around much longer. So I reached out to its founder, Michael, whom I had known for a long time. Actually, he has known *me* for a long time. He watched me grow up and loved my family, especially my grandfather. He held my grandfather in very high regard and always asked about him every time I talked to him. Even in the conversation I had with him about the chamber, he'd ask how my grandfather was doing and how much he just loved that man. He confirmed the chamber was struggling, and he was thinking a leadership change would be the solution. I asked him, "Do you have ideas on who could be a new leader?" What's interesting about this is that I asked this question because I was quite certain I knew the answer. I just didn't want to volunteer myself. I didn't know how to lead a chamber of commerce or any nonprofit for that matter, but I knew if he said my name, I knew with his support, I wouldn't mind giving it a shot. And as I expected, I was right. I let him know that I was open to it but would need his help, and he was in.

Michael, the chamber's current Executive Director, and I met about the transition for me to become the new Executive Director. I spoke at a scholarship event earlier that year, and the then-executive director was impressed with my presentation, so he asked me to speak at their gala being held the following month. At first, I was very honored. Here I was, only 27 years old at the time, and I was asked to be a keynote speaker for a gala! I was so excited. However, when I arrived at that event, I realized why I was tapped to be the speaker. Yes, I had a reputation in the community as a great, well-spoken young, and inspiring speaker. However, this event was mainly geared towards business owners, professionals, and influencers. Not the traditional community or church event, which had always been my preferred audience. The large hotel banquet room was barely half full, and the event was clearly not well put together. I realized I was a last-minute choice, but I took advantage of the opportunity anyway, as I love to speak, especially when I can spread the message to large audiences. Now, I should have expected a small attendance because of what the chamber was going through, but I had been caught up in the hype of speaking at a gala. In a meeting soon after the event, the chamber's current leader agreed to present me to the board to become the new Executive Director. He felt that with his role as a minister in the church and other endeavors, it would be best for him to step down anyway.

All of the individuals on the board were my parent's age or older. Some of them watched me grow up. "How is this shy young man going to grow this chamber?" is what I felt them thinking about me when I entered the room. But Michael always believed in me. He had watched me grow and seen me speak at church events, and from his perspective, he felt I could lead anything. He told me that someday he was going to be my campaign manager. I never mentioned to him or even gave it a thought that I would ever run for office. Regardless of how Michael thought of me, the board of the Black Chamber didn't feel the same way. I should not have been surprised when the board rejected the proposed change during its board meeting.

I called Michael after I left the meeting to tell him the news. He had a feeling this was going to happen as well. He said, "Start your own." I am so grateful for his confidence in me. He was definitely in my life for a reason, even if it was just for a short season. He said he would show me what he learned when he visited other cities that had a Black chamber. I met with him a couple of times and still didn't have much of a starting point after those meetings. This could be another reason why the chamber was struggling. It appeared he didn't have a grasp on how to run a chamber either, despite traveling to other cities to learn. Shortly after a few meetings with him, he informed me that he had accepted a new position with the state. His new role consumed much of his time and left little to no time to continue to mentor me. I was so frustrated that he talked me into doing this and then left me hanging. He had me so motivated to do this, and now what? But something inside of me told me to keep going. I thought this could be the opportunity I could use my voice for a purpose. I once heard that nothing can stop a man or a woman who will not quit, so I committed to doing everything I could to figure this out on my own.

THE BIRTH OF A VISION

I began to have a craving building up inside of me. I was mad, embarrassed, and a little discouraged. But I used that as fuel rather than water for the fire that was burning up inside of me. I became intensely focused on figuring out how to start a chamber of commerce. I went online and researched the legal structure and what type of entity a chamber needed. There were several hours spent on my couch with my laptop filling out the 501c6 application, working on a budget, bylaws, and learning how a chamber even works. I attended other chamber events and other networking events and studied how they were set up. Of all people in my social network, my dad discovered a Hispanic chamber of commerce in Utah. He was attending networking events as well, trying to build his networking marketing business, and discovered this organization. This was great because there was already another ethnic chamber established, and I could possibly model my efforts after them. So, my dad and I attended their next networking event. He introduced me to a couple of their founders that he had met, and I shared with them that I was looking to start a Black chamber. They heard my passion, and instantly, I gained their support. They shared how they were structured and what documents were required. They were so supportive of walking me through the steps. They brought me in as their friend, and I'll never forget hanging out with the original leaders at their business conference, discussing, dreaming, and scheming what could be and how they would help me. I had all the confidence in the world at that point. If I just followed what they told me to do, and as leaders of one of the strongest chambers in the state at the time, I felt assured of success having them as a mentor. They lit a fire under me, even more than the old board of the other Black chamber. They inspired me and encouraged me to believe that I could do this and that I had all the support I needed. It took two years for me to officially launch the new chamber, but I stayed committed to the task the whole time. It didn't feel like it was two years, though. There were times when I was impatient or frustrated. Michelle and I had just begun dating during this time. She asked me, "Why would you even put yourself through this?" She reminded me that I didn't have to do this. It's not paying me anything. The passion was there for me to rise up and carry on, though. And she felt it and supported me through it, and has been by my side ever since.

In August of 2011, we held our first event. The event was a community BBQ in the park. I didn't know how to find Black businesses in Utah, so my hope was to attract them to the chamber by hosting an event like this. Zions Bank helped support the other minority ethnic chambers, so I went to them for support. My first meeting didn't go so well. I felt like I had the basics down of how a chamber functions, but I didn't know how to sell it. I didn't realize how important that was until I sat down with a bank asking for sponsorship. I really didn't under-stand what sponsors would be looking for. They asked me what my goal was for the chamber and how I intended to support Black small businesses. They asked if I knew how many Black small businesses there were in the community. Embarrassingly, I didn't have answers to any of those questions. At the time they asked, it made sense to have those answers. Michael gave me a list of Black businesses that he discovered, and my only plan was to get that list of members and find more Black businesses. But I didn't know how to grow them other than connect them to each other through networking. I still had a lot of learning to do. Their response wasn't a no, but not a not yet, which I appreciated.

I reached back out to the Hispanic chamber leadership and asked for guidance on asking for sponsorship. They walked me through how they support their members and community and why their sponsors are engaged. It all started to make more sense to me. They showed me how to build the foundation of an operation that would attract initial sponsors. Following their instructions, I went back to the bank six months later, and I got a yes! From there, I was able to move forward with the community BBQ. I got a local band, served hot dogs and hamburgers, found another sponsor for drinks, brought dominoes and cards to play, and received donations to give out prizes. I didn't want to show the community that I was competing with the other chamber, so I didn't put "chamber" in our name. I thought of a different name that worked in the meantime, ACCEL, African-Americans Advancing in Commerce, Community, Education, and Leadership (I know. It seemed cool at the time!). People didn't really buy into the fact that I wasn't trying to compete, however. Hell, I couldn't even sell myself on that strategy. What I believed, however, is that I learned how a chamber, particularly a minority ethnic chamber in Utah, should operate, and I didn't think the current Black chamber had that same vision.

Although very few Black businesses attended, I did gain a lot of support from the community. I had over 200 people show up – friends, family, church members, and members of the community interested in learning about ACCEL. The board of directors I selected didn't have much or any experience in participating on a board or even in a non-profit organization. They were mainly just supporters of the cause and were put on paper to make the organization legal. I had Michelle, my dad, a couple of friends, and one business owner as members of the board. I just had the basic requirements to operate, and we began learning along the way. The community BBQ was a huge success in my eyes. It was the momentum I needed to keep me encouraged, committed, and excited about what was to come. My vision was still small in the beginning, admittedly. At least compared to what the chamber looks like now. Utah has a very small Black population, so I knew the business population was going to be significantly smaller, if not the smallest, of any other community. The need, however, was still there, so I felt this could be something that could be successful part-time, and this could be the vehicle I was looking for to use my voice.

REFLECTION

"Opportunities are not lost. They are just found by someone else."

I used to wonder what would have happened if I didn't agree to lead the chamber and not follow through with starting my own; where I would be now? Would I still be looking for a purpose? Would my passion have faded away? From that point, I learned to at least hear out any opportunity that comes to me. Have you missed out on an opportunity you now wished you hadn't? You may not know when something is presented to you that will change your life forever. So as the saying goes, always stay ready, so you never have to get ready. What do you need to do now so you're prepared when the right opportunity comes to you?

10

PASSION: EVERY DAY I'M HUSTLIN'

"Be passionate and move forward with gusto every single hour of every single day until you reach your goal."

– AVA DUVERNAY

FROM SPITE TO FIGHT

IT WASN'T until 2012 that the other Black Chamber officially dissolved. However, people continued to hear about two different Black Chambers, and they had concerns. Rightfully so. I didn't like the fact there were two chambers, but I couldn't understand why the other chamber was determined to continue even though it had lost much of its credibility, the support of its original founder, and most of its sponsors. Being mostly shy and introverted, I didn't like the drama and tried to avoid it, but many times it met me head-on for me to work through it. Some of its leadership, including the executive director, met with me a few times, looking for ways to partner or even merge. I welcomed it. I thought it would be great, but it wouldn't happen if it was for me to step down. I was determined to show them and the rest of the community that I could lead and bring success to this organization. After a few events, I grew a vision of what the chamber could become, and it would mean a totally different direction than what the former Black Chamber leadership was moving towards. Consequently, the two organizations never came together, and the first Utah Black Chamber of Commerce closed its doors. So in 2014, we changed our name to the Utah African-American Chamber of Commerce, still remaining hesitant in taking over the name Utah Black Chamber of Commerce.

I spent several years learning how to grow not only a chamber of commerce but a Black one, specifically in the state of Utah. I started with nearly nothing but support from friends, family, and the Hispanic Chamber. All I had was my current network, which wasn't very big, especially for a purpose such as this. While they were there for me, I felt like I was pretty much on my own for a while working the chamber. The membership was slowly growing, and more corporate sponsors were coming on board, but it was still quite the process. I tried different types of networking events to attract people to the chamber. We held evening networking events and luncheons, and I tried a breakfast event a couple of times. I was looking for the best time for our community to get together. No matter what type of events I tried holding, the attendance remained small. I was beginning to realize, and even empathize, with what the old chamber had experienced. The difference for me, however, was that I had mentors surrounding me to help me navigate the different circumstances I was encountering and keep me motivated.

Supporters saw my work ethic and felt my passion, so they continued to believe in me. My vision continued to grow as I kept trying new things. I was beginning to understand what this organization could really do for the community. It took about five years for me to grow in my leadership and show the community this organization was here to stay and that I was the right guy to lead. By year five, I was able to attract stronger community leaders to the board of directors and get their buy-in. The board began to challenge me with initiatives and ideas on how we should grow. At first, it was hard because I wasn't used to that. But I realized this was what I wanted. This is what I needed and what the chamber needed. It needed more minds and ideas beyond mine.

WHY A BLACK CHAMBER IN UTAH?

Utah's Black community was barely under 1% of the state's population. When Michael was working with me to start the chamber, he shared a list of just over 100 Black-owned businesses. Based on those numbers, one might ask, why was I doing this? Would it even be worth the effort to start an organization with such a small population? I thought about my friends leaving Utah when they graduated high school. The Black community was a revolving door, with people coming in and out of Utah. Utah was not considered a destination for people of color. The Chamber was regularly receiving calls from people relocating to Utah inquiring if Utah was a safe space for them. They wanted to know if there was a church there for them, a barbershop or a salon for them, and good schools for their children. For single Black professionals, it was even more difficult. The social life in Utah is a lot different than the ones found in cities many of the individuals were coming from, and it can take a while to adjust. Unfortunately, many don't have that type of patience, especially when they are having a hard time connecting to the community. At the beginning when people asked me these questions, it was hard for me to respond and sell Utah. I shared my experiences, but by not having children of color or growing up in a more diverse environment, I struggled through some of these types of conversations. I needed more people around me to gain their insight. It was more than just growing our small Black businesses. The chamber had to focus on the whole community. If we wanted more businesses in our community, we had to work to ensure our community felt safe and welcomed enough to know they could reside, grow and thrive.

As the chamber gained more visibility, more companies began joining the chamber. Their goal was to connect to diverse local talent. I seized the opportunities as they came. If I could get the community together and have representatives from these companies there as well, they would see us within our environment and better understand how to connect, which would hopefully lead to them finding the talent they were looking for.

IMPACT WITH MOTOWN

The annual community BBQ was doing well, but I still wasn't satisfied. It began to become more of a reunion than an impactful event, but I wasn't sure what the next step would be to expand it. I thought about doing a business expo, but we were still struggling to find enough Black businesses that would join the chamber and engage with us for an event like that. I thought about even changing the BBQ to a different event entirely, but I was afraid of losing the support we already had.

In 2016, I received a phone call from a gentleman who was hosting free concerts at the downtown amphitheater. The concerts featured local talent each week. He found out about the chamber from my dad, as they are fellow musicians and have seen each other throughout the community. Dad, once again, seemed to have the connection at the right time. Jeff learned about the BBQ and had a proposal. The chamber and his organization had a mutual relationship with a band that performed a high-energy Motown show. He wondered if there was a possible collaboration between the concerts and our BBQ. I am always open to opportunities to try new ideas. Both organizations had good reputations, so it was worth a shot. That August, Excellence in the Community and the Utah African-American Chamber of Commerce came together to produce a community BBQ and Motown Show in downtown Salt Lake City. We gave out free BBQ and drinks to all the attendees before the show and invited our corporate sponsors to have a booth so they could interact with all the attendees. The collaboration was a huge success, drawing in a crowd several times larger than the smaller community BBQ in the park.

Each year, this event grew by the hundreds. The first time was the only time we gave away free food. After that, it didn't make financial sense anymore for us. Additionally, we began seeing a spike in Black-owned food trucks, so we transitioned to inviting them to the venue to sell their food. This change didn't stop attendance from growing. "The reunion" felt different this time. It felt impactful. We witnessed people of all backgrounds come together for a good time. How can you go wrong with Motown and BBQ? You can't. We didn't. It was so right. That event expanded our influence and introduced us to so many more people who wanted to engage with the chamber. The energy was something unlike anything that I felt before. I thought about my friends who had left Utah for a better diverse environment. I guarantee they would have stuck around longer if they felt what I felt at this event. An attendee wrote an email to Jeff: *"I am a police officer who loves music and diversity. Sometimes it is hard to find those things in Salt Lake City. That night I was able to experience both. That band that night (Changing Lanes) was awesome. The crowd that night was diverse and awesome. The music was fantastic. It was a blast watching the crowd and getting to know some new people. I am not a very religious person, but I believe I mentioned to you that that night was a spiritual experience for me, watching everyone get along and have fun together. Thank you for the effort in putting together this wonderful program. I look forward to more Excellence in the Community."* Within three years, the show grew to nearly 8,000 attendees. The event had to shut down due to the pandemic, but after the world became safer, we put the event back on in 2021, and the attendance has quickly grown back into the thousands again.

DIVERSITY AFTER FIVE

The board and I got together to expand on our success by learning more about what was going on around the country. One of the events we discovered happening in other parts of the country was First Friday. Every first Friday of the month, Black professionals would gather to connect and socialize. This helped the new residents of the community identify and get acquainted with their new environment. New residents of Utah had been experiencing challenges in connecting to other residents of color. One of the great things about Utah is we are all integrated. From early history, the military and railroad jobs located Black soldiers and workers throughout the valley and not isolated to one part of the city, as in some other states. However, with such a small diverse population, it has been challenging to locate Utah's diversity since it was just a little sprinkle throughout the state. Chamber leadership liked the idea of First Friday as a solution to this problem. To take it a step further, we wanted to create an event where our community would dress in formal attire and "celebrate us." One of our leaders came up with a theme, and we would host the event during Black History Month. In 2015, our inaugural First Friday, Evening in Harlem, was born.

Evening in Harlem celebrated the Harlem Renaissance, and we encouraged attendees to wear the attire of that era. With a jazz band and a casino, the event became a huge hit. We didn't charge attendees for entry as we gained full sponsorship and focused on this being an outlet for our community to come together. However, we quickly realized an opportunity we were missing. People loved the event so much that they planned for it to be an annual event. Evening in Harlem exceeded our expectations. It introduced us to more supporters of the chamber. Some attendees had never heard of the chamber until hearing about this event and were excited that there was something like this to bring us together. The following year, we charged for the event to support our community initiatives, and the attendee size doubled. The need was evident. An event like this didn't exist in our community, and people were hungry for something like this. The attendees doubled every year for three years, capping out at nearly 600 attendees. Because of that, we saw an opportunity to launch a 501c3 to focus on programming to further develop our community and use Evening in Harlem as our fundraiser.

For a few years, we lost sight of First Friday since the community BBQ and Evening in Harlem were doing so well, and I had limited bandwidth as the main "volunteer" without additional staff. However, I knew we needed to stay more consistent with our events. We were holding monthly luncheons, but attendance was always a struggle, and it wasn't delivering the impact we were hoping for. So we decided to bring back the original plan of hosting a monthly First Friday beginning in July 2019. Even though it was a holiday weekend, the event was still successful. Over half of the attendees shared that they had been in Utah for less than two years. With the success of the signature events, First Friday continued to be successful each month, attracting 60-80 people each month, with several new people attending each month. Membership began to grow significantly from individuals, nonprofit organizations, small businesses, and larger corporations. We were beginning to build a community. In 2018, we wanted to become a more inclusive organization for all of the Black community, and we changed our name to the Utah Black Chamber of Commerce, now comfortable and strong enough to say that we are this organization and the conversation about another Black Chamber had entirely faded away.

A MAN ON A MISSION

I went without pay the entire time as the leader of the Utah Black Chamber for almost 13 years. Even when it grew to potentially even pay me, I wanted to make sure the foundation was so strong that we would be able to hire someone full-time. I believed I could make this organization successful. I wanted the organization to succeed so badly, I was willing to do whatever it took. Not just because the community needed it but to believe in myself–to actually have success with something. I was tired of feeling mediocrity in all things I strived for in my life. As I shared earlier, I started the chamber a little after I left network marketing. I had just gone through a divorce with my first wife a few months prior, and had to move back to my parent's house temporarily to get back on my feet. I was stagnating at my job and wasn't enjoying it much. I was pretty down on myself. The chamber gave me a spark. It gave me hope, and I was good at it. I discovered new talents and skills I didn't realize I had. I began to wake up with a purpose. This was the vehicle I was looking for. My mind was overstimulated with ideas, visions, and dreams of what could be. At the time, I didn't fully consider who I would truly become during this journey. I knew what had to be done and what it was going to take. The influence I have today wasn't planned or expected. But I was passionate about what the chamber could be. There may have been a little spite in the beginning to give me the fuel I needed to show the naysayers what I was capable of. I knew where I could take not only this organization but the entire Black community. My vision continued to grow bigger as the chamber continued to grow.

REFLECTION

Passion. Have you found it? If you haven't, what is constantly going through your mind? So much so that you can't shake it? What calls out to you?

"If you want a thing bad enough to go out and fight for it, to work day and night for it, to give your time, your peace, and your sleep for it.

If all you dream and scheme about it, and life seems useless and worthless without it.

If you'll gladly sweat for it, and fret for it, and plan for it, and lose all your terror of opposition for it.

If you'll simply go after that thing that you want with your capacity, strength, and sagacity; faith, hope, confidence, and stern pertinacity.

If neither cold, poverty, famine or gaunt, sickness and pain; a body or brain can't keep away from that thing you want.

If in darkness and grim you beseech and beset it, with the help of God, YOU WILL GET IT!"

—LES BROWN

11

INFLUENCE: I CAN ONLY BE ME

"If you think you're too small to make a difference, you've never spent the night with a mosquito."

– AFRICAN PROVERB

BUILDING AND GROWING a nonprofit organization for the smallest demographic in the state in the most philanthropic state in the country is no easy feat. The most important ability I had to learn was establishing and building relationships. You would think someone with an introverted background wouldn't master this ability as well as I have, but I would argue it's one of the main reasons I am so strong at this ability. There are several qualities of an introvert that generally qualify them as terrific leaders. I thought I had to get outside my comfort zone to grow this organization, meeting people and trying to sell chamber memberships to small businesses. But that wasn't working for me. Looking back, it was the same problem I had in the network marketing business. I was compromising who I was as a person, and I needed to simply trust the person I was, the person Michael saw in me, and allow that individual to lead. Once I became comfortable with who I was as a person, everything began to come together.

AMBITIOUSLY LAZY

"It's okay to be a copycat as long as you're copying the right cat."

Working full-time and going to school for my master's degree, I didn't have a lot of time to build a nonprofit organization from scratch. I also hated researching. Research and paying attention to detail are not my strengths at all. I prefer to find others already doing what I am trying to do, connect, and watch them. The Utah Hispanic Chamber was one of my best mentors in the beginning. They showed me nearly everything to get set up. They showed me all their bylaws, how they were structured, who they looked for in their board, and the purpose behind all of their events. I attended all of their events; luncheons, evening networking events, conferences, golf tournaments, and any training they held. Knowing the purpose behind all of them, I was able to attend with intention, and I observed their whole run of show – their set up and take down of the event, how the leaders interacted with the guests, and how the executive director spoke to the audience as being the host. I took note of the number of people that would be required to have an event at certain levels of capacity as well as the type of people to support these events. I noticed there was a particular personality that did really well at the check-in desk, another personality who thrived at the set up of the event, and the type of host that engaged attendees. After about a year of attending events, I felt like I had the secret sauce of any type of event, but it took longer for me to find the ingredients for that sauce, meaning the people.

The Hispanic Chamber events were also low-hanging fruit for new corporate members. These companies were also supporting diversity, so it was easier to sell the Black Chamber membership to them than to companies who have yet to support a diverse business organization. So, while I was a student of the game, I was also applying a lot of what was taught to me when connecting with companies to become potential members of the Black Chamber. Over time, people began to recognize me and see my commitment to the process, which they highly valued. Even though it was exhausting for me to attend so many networking events, the reward was getting my name and the chamber's name out there in the community.

As the chamber began to grow, I started observing bigger organizations. Larger organizations operate differently than smaller ones. Not just because they have more staff and larger budgets, but because they have a larger influence in their community and leverage their voice to bring change beyond their mission by either supporting other organizations they align with or engaging with state and federal legislators. These organizations also may have multiple entities to expand their purpose. Sometimes tax or entity structures may not always work as the platform grows and you are being exposed to more opportunities to serve your community.

IT'S NOT YOU, IT'S ME

Working alone was not an issue for me. I have always enjoyed working on my own. I never liked group projects. It's one of the few things that test my patience. So, in the beginning, I was not worried about forming a team yet. I didn't want to put people through the torture of trying to work with me when I wasn't even sure what I was doing yet. My poor board members were more cheerleaders than anything. They would volunteer for things when I asked them, but I was not good at asking for help. I was intensely focused on just getting done what my mentors asked me to do. As long as I had a roadmap, I was good. It took a few years before I learned to delegate and allow people who wanted to serve to become more engaged. To this day, I still struggle with delegation. I have to remind myself to pull my head up so I can see the people around me who are ready to be in the trenches with me.

Other supporters and influencers respected my work ethic and joined the chamber because they saw my energy and passion. People are attracted to those that just work hard. I wasn't looking for any attention. Finding the spotlight is not one of my strengths, but I am able to bring the spotlight to the chamber simply through my production. The chamber began receiving media attention once they began to hear about the Black Chamber's impact. I had no experience in contacting the media and asking to come to this event or seeking an opportunity to get on the air for something. People just started asking me to be on air, TV, radio, and podcasts because of our impact. I have several pages of links to news articles, TV footage, commercials, radio interviews, and podcasts that I kept on file. The visibility of the chamber continued to grow due to impact, not me trying to be famous.

BE INSPIRING

"Those times when you stay up late, and you work hard; those times when you don't feel like working — you're too tired, you don't want to push yourself — but you do it anyway. That is actually the dream. That's the dream. It's not the destination, it's the journey. And if you guys can't understand that, what you'll see happen is that you won't accomplish your dreams, your dreams won't come true, something greater will."

— KOBE BRYANT

The USA Basketball Team had dominated in the Olympics until the late 80s when all of a sudden other countries developed stronger teams and became more competitive. The gold medal was no longer a gimmie for the USA team. The team had always consisted of college players representing our nation's basketball, but in order to win in this more competitive environment, leadership decided it was time to bring in the big boys, the NBA players. In 1992, the Dream Team was announced. This team had the best NBA players at the time: Michael Jordan, Magic Johnson, Karl Malone, John Stockton, Charles Barkley, and other NBA All-Stars. The Dream Team brought USA basketball back to dominance again.

At the same time, the NBA was becoming more competitive and more physical. Athletes were getting faster and stronger, putting more of a physical toll on their bodies. Players would consider not participating in the Olympics to rest their bodies. The NBA also began attracting international players developing in the U.S. and would return to their home country to represent the world games. For three consecutive Olympics in the early 2000s, the USA team was no longer dominant. They even brought in younger NBA players like LeBron James, Carmelo Anthony, and Dwayne Wade. Yet, they were still falling short. What needed to happen to bring back the gold? The answer? Kobe Bryant.

Kobe was a veteran in the league at a young age and already a champion. He had a different mindset than anyone else in the league. When he joined the Olympic team, he brought a different level of intensity. During practice, he didn't hold back. He dived for loose balls, played hard on defense, and disrupted his teammates practicing against him. Players were intimidated by him. They didn't know how to connect with him in the beginning. One night, all the players went out to the club and stayed out until the early morning. When they arrived back at the hotel around 4:30 in the morning, they saw Kobe Bryant coming out of the elevator with his gym clothes on and workout gloves on his way to work out. Players thought he was crazy at first, but it set the tone going forward.

Over time, more players began to get up earlier, felt it inspired them to take things more seriously, and began to work harder. In practice, they practiced harder. In the gym, they worked out harder. They all began to push themselves more. After that, every summer in Las Vegas, the team was more focused. They spent four summers together, learning more about each other and practicing harder. It went beyond just a bunch of NBA All-Stars showing off their skills in front of the world; it was a team of the best NBA talent who wanted the gold medal more than anything. Their inspiration was drawn from the leadership of Kobe Bryant, who accepted nothing less than a gold medal. In the NBA, he accepted nothing less than a NBA Championship. Making the playoffs wasn't good enough for him. In the Olympics, winning a medal wasn't good enough. He was asked to join the team to win the gold, and he was willing to do whatever it took to help the team to win the gold medal for the USA Basketball Team. In the 2008 Beijing Summer Olympics, the USA team brought the gold medal back to its country.

"Hustle in silence. Let your success make all the noise."

— FRANK OCEAN

To inspire others, you need to have that "Black Mamba" mentality. Show people how badly you want your dream and that you are willing to do whatever it takes to get it. Whether they are on your team, in the community, or just on the sidelines watching, you'll inspire people simply by your passion to grind. When the fire grew in me to grow the Black Chamber to become the best chamber in the state, I didn't publicly announce what I really wanted. I didn't blast on social media what my ultimate goal was for the Black Chamber. I allowed my work ethic to show that there is not only a need for a Black Chamber in Utah, but the organization's voice is going to become a strong voice for the Black community. I was tired of the perception Utah had about its diversity. Being a Utah native, I was annoyed and disappointed that people wouldn't give Utah a chance. How do we expect to grow this community if no one is willing to stay and put in the effort to make Utah a place for the Black community and all communities of color? I knew I couldn't talk or sway people into believing in this vision. I had to show them. I had to prove to everyone, including people in the non-Black community, that this place is for everyone, and here is what we need to do for that to happen.

What great leaders understand is that the more responsibility you take, the more control you have over your destiny. Don't allow others to try to influence you otherwise. This is your goal. Your passion. Your mission. You have to inspire others to believe in it. You have to get others to buy into your vision and the best way to do that is to show them. Your belief, your passion, and your work ethic will become contagious. It will be motivating. It will be inspiring. On many occasions, I played the role of not only the executive director of the organization, but also the administrator, the marketing team, the finance team, and the volunteer. I was setting up events. I was breaking them down. Nothing was too small for me because there was nothing too big for me to accomplish. I was willing to do whatever it took.

VALUE MY INFLUENCE

I've often seen how much people value their position or title they have in a job and place so much focus on what that role brings them rather than what they bring to that role. When change occurs, and they leave that role, you never hear of them again. Hence, their title defined who they were. I've never been tied to the title. I've only been tied to the impact I make. A position doesn't make the leader, the leader makes the position. I never bothered chasing titles because titles are only temporary. Impact is eternal. Impact is what people remember. Back in 2014, the chamber was in a transitional time and needed more board members. We had a temporary executive director in place, and I was moving to the board. I was looking to be in a more supportive capacity (only to find out later the timing was not right). As we were making decisions about the executive committee, there was debate about chair and vice chair. To make the decision easier, I volunteered to be secretary. The executive director was shocked. "Why on earth would you choose that role?" He asked. I responded that no matter which position I take, I'll bring the same impact. I'm not worried about the position I have. It won't affect the work I will accomplish.

When you let go of the title and focus on who you are and what you bring to the table, living with purpose is so much more achievable. I'm seeking to expand my vision beyond the influence of the chamber, utilizing all of my platforms to accomplish my mission and building other leaders in the process. It's important that I leave my ego at the door and become a doorstopper. I want to be able to leave the door open for others to succeed in their own light. In John Maxwell's book, *Five Levels of Leadership*, he shares what leadership level you should strive for to establish a legacy. The first level is position, which is the lowest level. This is the level where your focus is the title or role you are playing in life – husband, wife, manager, president, etc. People only follow you because of your position, so there is an obligation. Would they follow you if you didn't have the title? That's the question you have to ask yourself. If people would follow you because they want to, then you've advanced to the next level of leadership, permission. How do you get permission? John writes, "People don't care how much you know until they know how much you care." To receive permission, you must show you care. You cannot become a doorstopper if you don't know the doors that need to be opened to make an impact.

This leads to the next level of leadership, production. This is the leadership level where I began. I was never looking to lead. Remember, I was surprised when I was notified I received a leadership scholarship for college. I had never led anything up until then. But when I am passionate about something, I put my all into it. My grandfather was a very hard worker, and that was instilled into me. I worked hard to accomplish the goals I committed myself to. The media coverage, commercials, and influence were a result of the growth of the chamber. People respected the organization for what it is and what it does for our community and others. I am still surprised to this day when people I have never met before approach me to share that they have watched the chamber and have watched what I have accomplished and are inspired and grateful for the impact. This let me know that my vision is coming true little by little, and that it's not always going to have to be me to carry out its purpose. Others have embraced the vision as well. This is leadership level four. People follow you because of what you have done for them personally. In the beginning, leading the chamber wasn't about changing lives for me. I wanted to develop a resource hub for the community. Why I didn't think that would change lives, I don't know. I guess I didn't fully understand the impact it could bring to the community until others shared their experiences with me. I count my blessings every day for this opportunity and know that my journey is not over. There is so much more that can be done, will be done, and there will be many others who will be on this journey with me. I'm still aiming for that last level of leadership – pinnacle leadership. "People follow because of who you are and what you represent." I have represented many roles, but now it's time to represent James Jackson, III. Defining that person is the next step for me.

MANAGING EMOTIONS AND ENERGY

One trait I realized about myself is that I rarely display my emotions. I have always managed my emotions pretty well and keep my behavior pretty regulated when it comes to business. Circumstances don't rattle me much. Often people don't know when I am stressed, anxious, or even nervous. I can stay even keel. There have only been very few times where people have seen me angry. I also enjoy being alone. I need that time to recover and recharge. I spend half of my life by myself. From 10 PM to 8 AM is my time. I am winding down, sleeping, and rising and preparing for the day. I like getting up early and having alone time while the rest of the family sleeps. It allows me to prepare for the day of interacting with people. It's the main reason why I have the energy I have throughout the day. When there has been too much interaction, you can find me at home afterward just staring at the TV, usually a rerun of something so my mind doesn't have to do much. I need more time to recharge.

LISTEN WITH INTENTION

The strongest ability of any leader is the ability to listen. Listening is an underrated skill today. With all of our devices giving us access to information and screens at will, we have developed the attention span of a goldfish. It has become more difficult for us to listen because we are easily distracted by so many things around us. Leaders are listeners and listen with intention. I paid attention to many CEOs that I am close with and watched them interact with people in the community. When they are talking to people, they show their undivided attention. They are not paying attention to their phones or what others around them are doing. They are looking at the person speaking to them and listening to every word. Not interrupting or changing the subject. They ask questions and are responsive.

Listening takes a lot of energy, which is another reason people don't listen well. Talking takes less energy than listening to someone. I've always been a pretty good listener. I would rather listen than talk. When speaking one-on-one with someone, people tend to open up to me and share more than they intend to at times. I work to create a safe space for them so they feel comfortable. There have been a few times where people have sat down with me, and minutes later, I am a counselor for them, or they become emotional during our conversation. One time, someone was running late to meet me at a coffee shop. This was the first time I met her in person. When she finally got settled in and began to talk to me, she just dumped all of her troubles of the day onto me and then began crying. I didn't mind it, but I don't know what to do when someone cries, especially if we just met. She apologized for crying, but she said it was nice of me to listen and allow her to vent for a minute. After she gained her composure, we got right to business, and because of our connection, she became a big ally for the chamber and a champion for anything I engaged in.

I also like to be open and transparent with people so they know exactly what my intentions are. A gift (and a curse) of introverts is that we are not ones for small talk or "fluffy conversations." I like to get to the point of the discussion. Becoming a business coach was a true test of my listening skills. After a two-hour session of intently listening to someone and guiding them to solutions was draining. My first few coaching sessions with a client, I came home and took a nap. It was exhausting, and it took a while to build up my endurance. However, I'm learning to become better at not allowing distractions in social environments when conversing with someone. I want to be able to 'listen like a CEO.'

REFLECTION

Servant leadership has always been the base of my influence. I like to be part of the boots of the ground amongst everyone doing the work. Author and speaker Jim Rohn says, "A service to many leads to greatness." The only way I know how to deliver impact is to be of service. As my impact grows, I hope to attract other servant leaders to follow me. When you are passionate enough about something, you want to understand how everything works. Then as your purpose grows, you are able to teach and empower others who are with you.

- What level of leadership do you feel you are at now? Are you focused more on the position?
- Do you feel you have permission from others to lead them?
- Have you produced the results that honor the level of respect for them to follow you?
- What opportunities do you have to have an impact on others?

12

ENDURANCE: CAN'T STOP, WON'T STOP

"I don't stop when I'm tired. I stop when I'm done."

– DAVID GOGGINS

WHEN YOU READ about living your dreams or pursuing your passion, you'll find that what is rarely discussed is the physical endurance necessary to achieve your desires. You can only go as far as your body can go, so if you're not taking care of yourself physically, no matter how much experience, wisdom, or skill you have, your health could still prevent success. Great physical endurance requires daily exercise, good nutrition, and sufficient sleep.

SMALL BUT MIGHTY

I have always been in good physical shape. I enjoyed playing all sports growing up. While I wasn't a star in any particular sport,

I still considered myself athletic. I had strong legs that allowed me to be fast and jump high, so basketball became my favorite sport. In high school, I was introduced to weightlifting. When I entered high school, I was 5'8" and less than 120 pounds. Needless to say, weightlifting really caught my attention. There were girls that I liked that were bigger than me! During my senior year, I had a chance to compete for the bench press record for my weight class. I was pretty confident in breaking the record, but what I didn't know was that there was someone else also trying to break the record. The record was 275 pounds, and I lifted 280 with ease. The next day, I saw my nickname, "Action Jackson," written on the board. I wish I had taken a picture of that board because it was just the next week that a different name appeared with 285 pounds written next to it. I couldn't believe it. Determined to get back on the board, I tried for the record again, which meant 290 lbs. I trained for a couple of weeks and thought I was ready. Several times over the next few days, I tried pushing that weight, but it was too heavy for me. Dejected, I gave up and gave myself props for having the record for at least a week.

Whether it's fitness or life, pushing through your peak is hard and a true test of not just your strength, but your will and desire to overcome. We resolve to maintain at that peak level or we begin to digress by discouragement. That's not what we want, though, is it? We want to keep going. We want to keep growing, so how do we find the motivation? It's in your passion. Your purpose. Staying in shape is a key element in accomplishing goals. Physically, you need sufficient health to attend events, make calls, network, and connect with people. Back to sports, I see the 400-lb. linemen on the football field who run through opponents, shedding blocks ,and chasing down the ball handler. They are not all muscle – there's a lot of fat on them, yet, they are nimble, flexible, and fast. Yes, they trained at a much higher level than most of us, but how badly did they want their dream to come true? Some wanted to play another position but were encouraged to move the line, which required putting on a significant amount of weight. My favorite football team is the Pittsburgh Steelers. There was one player on that team who was drafted as a tight end. Traditionally, tight ends are the largest receivers on the field. They may not be as fast as the wide receivers, but they are taller, stronger, and are also used as an additional offensive lineman to block. However, during his training, the coaches decided he was better suited to play the most important role on the offensive line – protecting the quarterback's blindside. This position required him to gain almost 100 pounds. Do you think all that weight was muscle? Not likely, but he still maintained his nimbleness and quickness to protect his teammates.

That player did what was ever necessary to live out his dream. It's a commitment to the process. On the other extreme, I was small in stature and shy, so I was easily picked on. For me, lifting weights was an answer for me to add more weight, become stronger, and become more confident with myself. From the end of high school to age 30, I put on 50 pounds, the majority of that weight being muscle. I had a high metabolism when I was young, so putting on weight was hard. I had to commit to a process. Once I hit a peak, I maintained my physique for a while. But once I got married, I began to let go a little bit. I played sports every now and then, but I wasn't consistently exercising. I became comfortable. Was I comfortable with myself, though? I was not. Exercising did more for me than staying physically healthy. It kept me mentally and emotionally healthy as well.

TAKING IT OUT ON THE WEIGHTS

As I grew older, life brought more challenges. The usual challenges when growing and becoming independent – starting a career, living on your own, and learning how to manage life in general. I always found exercise as my solace so I could keep moving and staying focused. Working harder on your passion isn't the only solution to rise above the challenges that come in life. It takes all of you, and all of you means your mental, spiritual, emotional, and physical capacity. Doubt sets in if you're not emotionally ready. If you've reached a mental peak or block, you have to identify paths to personal growth. But the foundation of all this begins with your physical body. If you're not feeling it physically, it impacts your mental and emotional strength. Exercise not only impacts your strength, mobility, and longevity, but if you need a boost of confidence, if you're not able to shake negativity out of your mind, or if you hit a mental block, a good sweaty workout can help you. Once I understood that, my daily workout meant a whole lot more to me than just putting on some weight and being in shape. My workouts change the trajectory of how I feel, how I think, and how I overcome challenges. When I am working out, yes, I am focused on the technique, but once I get into my rhythm, I let my mind go free and let it think about the things that are top of mind. Challenges that are giving me stress, problems I am having a hard time finding the answers for, or ideas I'm trying to work through–I allow my energy during the workout to help me get through my thoughts, my stress, my worries, and my problems.

MOST OF YOUR ENERGY IS FOUND IN THE KITCHEN

I love food. Plain and simple. I eat when I am down. Eating is standard for me when it comes to establishing a connection with someone, either over breakfast, lunch, or at social gatherings. I love to try all foods. Well, almost all foods. I don't know if I can eat bugs, no matter how they are prepared. As I got older and my metabolism declined, it became challenging to maintain my shape and my energy levels. Working out every day was no longer providing the results they used to. The six-pack abs were fading quickly. I realized that I had to start eating better if I wanted to maintain my shape. We are all built differently. Not everyone is going to have the same results from a particular diet plan, whether it's no carbs, vegetarian, or vegan. We each have different DNA, genetics, and shape. We can't expect our bodies to have the same results from a plan that someone has from that same plan. However, we all know what is not good for us – candy, chips, fried foods, and anything that is processed or has added sugars. I have a weakness for french fries and potato chips. It's hard for me to stay away from those. So I don't. But I eat in moderation. Maybe once or twice a month, I'll indulge. One of my mentors shared that you have to enjoy your diet in order to succeed. If you are not enjoying what you are eating, then you won't follow your plan for long. One way is to eat 80% healthy and have fun 20% of the time. Eat well at home and enjoy the food you want to eat while socializing or on vacation. We live in an immediate gratification society, wanting results immediately. The long-term or permanent results for your body won't happen immediately. Most people who lose weight fast end up putting it back on just as fast. However, if you "trust the process" and focus on the long-term plan, you will have better results.

At the end of 2021, I took some time off for myself and didn't follow any plan. I just ate! I had my french fries, fried food, potato chips, gummy bears, and even drank some whiskey. I scaled back a little bit from exercising and just relaxed. The past two years were very challenging and overwhelming, and I just wanted to not do or think about anything. In only a two-week period, I put on 15 pounds! I knew eating well was important, but that time showed me what happens if I'm not intentionally focused on my diet. I anticipated only gaining a few pounds, but fifteen pounds really threw me. I immediately felt guilty about my actions. The break from everything was definitely needed, and I decided I would commit to doing that every year, but I will never stop exercising ever again. When I saw that number on that scale, I began to feel that weight. The perception I had of myself even changed. I am usually not a vain person, but I started criticizing myself on how I looked. Then my body felt like it didn't want to move as well. See how much my mental game was impacted just by seeing that number on that scale? But it gave me a wake-up call and a new commitment.

At the beginning of the year, I went back to my plan, but with more focus, and also more focus on my exercise. I changed my workouts, started eating out less, and ate better at home. In three months, I dropped 10 pounds, and after another two months, I dropped five pounds, getting back to the weight I had before that winter break. During that span, new ideas began to form, and I developed a new energy for life. It was more than just feeling refreshed. I was hungry for more. I know I can lose more weight, but once again, once you reach that peak, it gets tougher, and you have to ask yourself, how bad do you want it? I have dropped as much as 17 pounds and have been adding and dropping weight since. Reflecting on what I really want out of life, I decided to be happy with the way I look, how I feel, and how much I want to enjoy life. Could I get more in shape? Absolutely. I know if I commit, I will make it happen. Is it worth it for me, though? Meh. I love food too much!

Additionally, my energy level wasn't the same as when I was younger. In order to maintain the level of energy needed to perform my best, what I consumed in my body impacted that as well. I attended a Tony Robbins event a few years ago and witnessed his energy level. He is unreal. I don't think he is human! He maintains high energy for the whole event, which includes twelve-hour days. He encourages water and snacks, and not a lot of heavy eating like a full meal. I didn't think I would make it. I am used to eating two to three full meals a day, and you want me to just snack the whole time? But I wanted the full experience and didn't want to miss what was being shared on the stage. After that event, I bought some of his books. In his first best-seller, *Unlimited Power,* Tony shares how he maintains a high level of energy. In one of the chapters, he shares his nutritional plan and what he researched about food. Water-rich foods are what he suggests to have in your diet the most – about 70%. Water-rich foods are mainly fruits and vegetables. Our bodies are made of mostly water and is the best natural cleanser, particularly when you add other nutrients that are found in fruits and veggies. He also suggests nuts and seeds as a source of protein. A lot of what we are seeing in today's society is "clean" eating. Plant-based and organic foods are the growing trends, not just for people that have to eat that way, but as a choice. I have always been a big meat-eater, but I don't eat it as much as I used to.

In 2021, I decided to have a physical. I can't recall the last time I had one. I rarely get ill. Catching COVID in March of that year was the first time I was sick in almost a decade. I never had as much as a cold or a fever until then. The pandemic showed me that checking your health should be more important than I was taking it. Overall, the doctor's visit went well, except for my cholesterol, which I feel is more genetic than my diet. Both of my parents have cholesterol challenges. The doctor provided me with a nutritional plan to follow and shared some insight about the foods I choose to ingest: red meat is high in cholesterol; pork can also lead to high blood pressure, and even poultry should be consumed lightly. Fish is a great source of protein, but you have to be careful about your mercury consumption. Fatty carbohydrates like fried foods and pizza are the "energy killers." Have you felt like you ate so much food that he first thing you want to do is take a nap? That's mostly related to the carbs you consumed. To keep your energy levels up, keep fruit and veggie snacks around the house and eat them first. Drink lots of water. As I stated, find the right nutrition plan for you, but if we want to perform at our maximum level each day, we need our energy.

YES, I DO SLEEP!

When people discover all that I am involved in, people ask if I have any time for sleep. Sufficient sleep is the only way I get anything done. Ever since I was little, sleep has always been a part of my health regime. When I was young, my parents never had to struggle to put me to sleep. Often, I would just go to bed on my own. Contrary to what people see, I love sleep. I love the time I spend in bed. Before I fall asleep, I think about the day I had and what I have for the next day. I use that time to prepare for keynotes or training I am scheduled to deliver. I reflect on my wins and what I can do better. I write down key highlights and what I learned. When I wake up, I write down what I'm grateful for and what I want to achieve for that day. On average, I spend about 7-8 hours in bed and about 6-7 hours of that time sleeping. This is the most important time of the day for me. Without a commitment to this time every night, including weekends, I am not as effective the following day as I would like to be. I understand struggling with a problem or challenge during the day that tests your thinking, ability, or experience. I don't like having to struggle because of a lack of sleep. To me, that's a lack of focus, passion, or intention. You're not living with purpose. Rarely are there moments in life where you have to sacrifice your sleep. We all sacrifice our time to rest based on our lifestyle or poor time management.

According to the National Sleep Foundation, healthy adults need at least seven hours of sleep per night. Babies, young children, and teens need even more sleep to enable their growth and development.[1] Many of us, unfortunately, sleep less than that. We live in such a fast-paced society, working long hours, and still want to find time for a social life. That kind of lifestyle catches up to you eventually and leads to less focus and desire to achieve your goals and more focus on just getting through the day. Without sufficient sleep, you don't have the energy to exercise, or focus on your eating habits. It's a domino effect. This is why sleep is critical to daily living. For me, too much sleep leads to laziness and loss of motivation. If I don't get enough sleep at night, I find time during the day for a nap. It doesn't make sense to me to "power through" if I am not in the right mindset. I'll spend just as much time getting myself refreshed, napping, and coming back to it, then trying to push through. A 15 to 30 minute nap is usually enough to give me the energy I need. I try not to nap too long. Too long of a nap is just as bad as too much sleep. I feel groggy and am too lazy to try to be productive. The key to good sleeping habits is not to overdo it or underdo it, just do it well.

KEEP YOUR DEVICES AWAY FROM YOUR BED

Some of us need a little help getting to sleep, so we get on our devices to watch something or get on social media. I found this to backfire for me. You can probably relate, but sometimes, I can go down a rabbit hole on social media, especially in bed. Either before I go to bed or when I wake up, I end up spending too much time and lose valuable sleep time or my morning routine time to take care of important tasks. I also watch a lot of TV. It's my downtime after work. I need time to recover, and I just like to sit. I mostly watch sports, but there are times when I find a movie or a series on a streaming app that captures my attention. There were many nights I found myself watching a series and had to watch the next episode and the next episode, and then it started getting good, so I watched the next episode. . . The next thing I know, it's extremely late at night, and I already know the next day is going to be a struggle. To stay focused on my goals, I resolved to keep devices away from the bed, so I wouldn't be tempted to pick them up. Instead, I use a journal and write down my thoughts. I don't spend a lot of time, but when you're ready to turn in for the night, you'll find it takes more energy to write down your thoughts than it is to allow devices to lead your thoughts. This will also add clarity to your life and purpose, whereas social media and television can damage or sway your thinking. Have you ever read something or watched something that led to a terrible night's sleep? Don't take that risk. Use a journal, read a book, or allow your own thoughts to take you down for the night.

SUCCESS IS FOUND IN YOUR DAILY ROUTINE

Over time, I recognized how I can reach my peak performance. With sufficient sleep and getting up on time, exercise in the morning, and intentional focus, I am ready for a highly successful day, and it happens more often than not because I live with purpose. It took a while for the habit to develop, but once it was formed into a habit, it soon became a lifestyle for me. When I don't commit or fail to finish my routine from 9 PM to 8 AM, I am not at my greatest. This is the only time of day I know that I have all to myself, so I take advantage of it. Most people will start their routine in the morning, but my routine begins when I go to bed, understanding the importance of getting sufficient sleep. When I lay down, I pick up my journal and reflect on the day. If there was a particular event, meeting, or interaction that stands out to me, I think about what I could have done better. I also think about the next day. What should I look forward to? How do I need to prepare? If I have a meeting or event or a keynote or training I am giving, I imagine the presentation in my head, combining anecdotes and lessons and structuring them for an effective delivery. Sometimes those thoughts can freak me out, and I have a hard time sleeping. This is a good moment to get up and begin writing down those thoughts until I have clarity and am relaxed enough to go to sleep. Before I know it, my alarm goes off at 5 AM. It used to be 6 AM, but I recognized that I needed more time in the morning. As my influence began to expand into different time zones, a 9 AM to start working wasn't early enough. I started having 8 AM meetings, and there's no going back to my routine if I have to cut it off. I'm kind of OCD that way.

I've moved on from my morning and now into my workday. I need as much time in the morning as possible to operate optimally for my family, community, and job. When that alarm goes off, there's no snooze for me. I get up. Even if I don't get enough sleep, I still get up. I never understood the snooze function. An alarm has already interrupted the REM sleep, so another nine minutes isn't going to help much. As a matter of fact, studies show that hitting the snooze button is not only ineffective for more sleep, it actually disorients your body and leads you to move more slowly in the morning. You are more effective getting up from less sleep than hitting the snooze button for more sleep. When that alarm goes off, I know whether I'm still sleepy or not, it's letting me know it's time to get ready for the day ahead.

To help me wake up, I began thinking about the day. What do I need to prepare for, and how do I prepare? I write down what I want to achieve for the day and what I'm grateful for. This sets the intention for me to go out and succeed. I throw on my gym shorts, socks, and shoes and go work out. My gym is at home. Over time, I acquired all the equipment and designed the space in my house for exercise. Working out for me is my daily coffee. I am not much of a coffee drinker. Working out wakes me up. Even if I'm tired, I still go to work out. I may not be as effective as I want to be during my workout, but it wakes me more than I was before. When I began this routine over 13 years ago, a friend of mine introduced me to P90X. This was when they were all on DVDs. I borrowed them and loved that workout. A little while after I completed the program, BeachBody developed an on-demand program online, which eventually turned into an app for your mobile and streaming devices. This gave me access to all of their workouts. Each time, a different program has helped me continue my routine and not let it get mundane. Every 90 to 120 days, I am starting a new workout program. I've also noticed a change in my body over the last three years. I've gained even more muscle and have maintained the same weight for the most part, which means I have become leaner as well. I work out seven days a week, using Sunday as a stretch or yoga day. Now that I am older, mobility, flexibility, and balance are more important to me than strength. However, even with a focus on those, increasing strength is still an outcome.

After I work out, my mind is clear, stress is reduced or eliminated, and I am ready for the day. While cooling down, I spend some time in devotion, reading my bible, listening to a talk, and praying. Spending time with God is something I have always valued. I credit Him with everything that has come into my life, good and bad. He has given me lessons as well as blessings, and I have worked to be equally grateful for both. God's Word always has a verse or story that I can reference when things are rough for me or if I am just looking for an answer to a particular issue. I may not attend church as regularly as I used to, but He is and always will be a constant in my life every morning. After my cool down and devotion time, I hit the shower and get ready for the day. Even if I'm not leaving the house, I get ready. It's a mental thing more than anything else. If I get ready for the day, well, I'm ready for the day. This doesn't mean I'm throwing on regular clothes if I'm staying home (I'm not putting on a suit like my grandfather!), but I'm "camera ready" and have some comfy clothes on.

Before I begin anything else for the day, I remove all distractions, and one of the biggest distractions for me is a house in disarray. So, I spend time cleaning up the kitchen, picking up the living area, usually from the mess of toys the dogs made around the house, and I make the bed. The house doesn't have to be spotless, but clean enough so it's not a distraction. I read an article about how making the bed impacts your psyche for the day. It's a sense of accomplishment that, while small, provides a sense of pride and fulfillment to encourage you to complete more small tasks throughout the day. So you can see how journaling, working out, cleaning the house, and making the bed the first part of the day puts me on the path for an incredible day. But I still have one more task to complete before starting my workday and that's either writing or reading.

For the last year, I spent about 30-45 minutes each day writing this book. If I'm not writing a book, I'm reading one. My mental game needs to have its own workout regime as well to have the endurance for me to grow. My goal is to have my routine completed by 8 AM. Sometimes, I may not finish by that time, and I'll take the extra time needed to complete everything if I don't have a meeting, but once I finish my routine, my mind is clear, I'm focused, and I am ready to tackle the day ahead. Imagine having that much accomplished before you even begin your day of work! How encouraging would you feel knowing you have already accomplished so much? When people ask me how I am able to do everything that I am doing and can be so busy, it is because of this 'bookend routine.' This daily constant gives me the physical and mental strength I need to focus and live my life with purpose.

REFLECTION

How do you currently get ready for the day? Think about the tone you set for yourself when you get up in the morning. How do you feel? What methods can you take to improve your overall mental, spiritual, and emotional strength? Some of us are more night people than morning people. I am not an expert in sharing which time is better for exercise. There are studies that support both times of the day. For me, I realize after a long day at work, the last thing I want to do is work out. Others feel the only way they can get in a workout is in the evening. Either way, a routine implemented into your lifestyle can help bring you to the mindset and find the inspiration and time to live out your purpose.

PART FOUR
LEGACY

13

PASSION: A COMMUNITY BUILDER

"If you're going to live, leave a legacy. Make a mark on the world that can't be erased."

– MAYA ANGELOU

THE UTAH BLACK Chamber was experiencing significant growth. From 2018 to 2022, the chamber grew by over 400%. The social justice movement of 2020 contributed to much of that. People from all over the state wanted to support our efforts and be an ally to the Black community. Opportunities were flying in, and I did my best to keep up with it all. Looking back, I don't think I was in denial that I was struggling, but I was in the moment and trying to live up to the servant leadership mentality that I inherited from my mentors. From the beginning, my goal wasn't to lead the chamber forever. I just wanted to build a solid foundation and pass it on to someone else. Naively, I thought that would only take five years, and there I was, 13 years in, still building that foundation. At the time, what I didn't realize was that I had built more than a foundation. I had built a legacy for myself. The chamber paved the way for so many other organizations, businesses, and individuals and significantly broadened the impact of the Black community as a whole. My vision grew even larger, and I sought more opportunities to impact Utah's overall diversity.

LIVING COLOR UTAH

A large financial firm approached Salt Lake City's leadership and shared that they are experiencing challenges retaining diverse talent. While they were the most diverse company in the state, they were experiencing a constant revolving door of diverse employees coming and going. What they discovered from the employees leaving was they weren't able to connect to their own community. While the company had a great diversity, equity, and inclusion strategy, they weren't able to control much of what happens when that employee goes home for the day. The company's leadership was hoping the city could help them by creating an event or a program to help diverse professionals, especially new ones who had just moved to Utah, to help introduce them to Utah's diverse community. The city's economic development team met with me, and we explored ideas. I pitched the idea of creating a website that included events, businesses, and programs from each of the diverse chambers in Utah. I knew of a program that could assist with all the integration and shared how much it would cost. They liked the idea and granted the initial funds to produce the web page. I met with the other diverse chamber leaders, and we created the brand Living Color Utah, in the fall of 2018. We all formed a website as a one-stop shop to connect to our organizations, events, and businesses. We also sought to share resources and other organizations in our community that could support professionals and their families. This collective helped us better collaborate and promote one another.

To better our efforts, we worked together to launch a diversity career fair. For three straight years, we hosted nearly 200 students and professionals to meet with roughly 50 companies from across the state seeking diverse talent. In of those years, we held a panel discussion for the employers to share best practices regarding hiring, retaining, and growing diversity. The career fair was put on pause during the pandemic, but there are plans to bring that career fair back by 2024.

One of the leaders of Living Color Utah pitched the idea of having an awards gala that recognized individuals and organizations making an impact in Utah's diverse community. This event would also introduce these leaders and their mission to a broader community. I thought it was a great idea, but I wanted to ensure this event attracted more than just the diverse community. We all are familiar with what's happening within our own communities. I wanted this event to be received by audiences who are not as familiar. A local business magazine, *Utah Business*, consistently recognizes people in the community, from CEOs, salespeople, emerging leaders, and women. They hold their awards luncheon once or twice a month, and their audience of CEOs, business leaders, and influencers, was exactly the audience we needed for this event.

I met with the editor-in-chief and pitched this gala. It would be their only evening event, and it would be a partnership with Living Color Utah. She loved the vision and would get the other magazine leaders on board as well. The first Living Color Gala was held in August 2019. Together, *Utah Business* and Living Color Utah honored 15 individuals and organizations that evening. We had exceptional attendance and support, and the event is now a staple event annually in our community. Since then, we have recognized nearly 60 individuals and organizations. The last two years, we have honored someone with the Cameron Russell Williams Award. Cameron was not only the inspiration for this event, but was also one of Utah's most passionate leaders around diversity. Cameron was a board member of the Utah Black Chamber, engaged in several other community organizations, and was a diversity officer for a tech company. He came to Utah after college to work for a financial firm, only expecting to be here for a couple of years before relocating to Texas–a familiar story I often heard from diverse professionals. They arrive here and don't expect to stay because they expect that it won't be a place for them. However, Cameron came here and saw the opportunities for growth, not only for himself but also for diversity. He became an influencer of change and made a significant impact in our community with his innovation, passion, and drive. Cameron passed away unexpectedly in 2021, but his legacy carries on within his family and local leaders within the diverse community.

BLACK UTAH: STORIES FROM A THRIVING COMMUNITY

In December 2020, I was approached via LinkedIn by a new publisher, Soul Excellence, that was looking for leaders throughout the world to share insight into how they led the community or their organization through the pandemic. I met with the founder, Kayleigh O'Keefe, and decided this would be a cool project to participate in. I had always wanted to write a book, and I thought this would be a great way to learn about the process and test my skills as an author. Prior to that time, I had written articles and a couple of blogs, but this time I would be in a book that would be sold to the public worldwide. That was pretty exciting! In January 2021, I, along with 24 leaders around the world, authored the book, *Leading Through the Pandemic: Unconventional Wisdom from Heartfelt Leaders.* We each wrote one chapter sharing how COVID impacted our organization and homelife and how we persevered and learned from that experience. Going through the process of participating in that project opened my eyes to the opportunity of writing my own book, but I wanted the book to be impactful. So, I went back to Kayleigh and shared my vision of what I wanted to do, and she agreed to partner with me.

Beginning in May of that year, I dove in. I was tired of the narrative of Black Utah. Media was sharing experiences that negatively impacted the perception of what it's like being Black in Utah. While the population is small and there is still so much work to be done for the state to be more welcoming, I wanted to share what people are doing to make that happen and how Black Utahns reside and thrive in a predominantly white state. So, I went out and interviewed dozens of people and couples, leaders and emerging leaders, business people, creatives, religious and community leaders, and influencers from the Black community. I tried to get a wide enough diaspora so when people read this book they would find someone to relate with. I also wanted to introduce the community to other leaders. Many of us joke around that we are part of the STP club, the Same Ten People. Every Black History Month or event around the Black experience, the community will typically call on the same few individuals every time. My hope was that after reading this book, the STP Club would dissolve! After several months of interviews and writing, the Utah Black Chamber published the book, *Black Utah: Stories from a Thriving Community* in February of 2021. I intentionally wanted to release the book during Black History Month to get as much exposure as possible. We began selling copies at all of our events, some of our community partners added the book to their retail shelves, and universities and libraries made the book available for people to read as well.

The book did *exactly* what I had wanted it to do. The STP didn't necessarily dissolve all the way, but people began identifying more influencers in the Black community. As the Black community continues to grow, people are beginning to see more Black leaders making an impact. I would argue that even though we are small, we are mighty. We have such strong leaders who desire to bring change to this community, and I can call on them at any time to partner, collaborate, and even lead many efforts. I hear about other Black communities in other states and the challenges they face. They are not nearly as connected as the community here in Utah. I know once people are introduced to any of the leaders, they will soon be introduced to most of the Black community. Utah has this culture where everyone is within two to three degrees of separation from one another. It's easy to learn about one another and what communities are doing. Many of the leaders in Utah have an "open door policy," meaning they are not out of reach or out of touch to connect with. These strengths played a significant factor in my success of building the Black Chamber and my platform. I shared with people often that I don't think I would have been able to accomplish in Utah in the amount of time I did in any other state. I believe the future is bright for Utah's Black community.

THE BLACK MUSEUM

In the fall of 2020, a local museum board member reached out to me about curating a Black museum. The museum had a 3,000-square-foot space available, and thought it would be a great opportunity to curate a museum that shares the history, experience, and community of Black Americans nationwide and locally. I never thought about a museum to educate people about diversity, but it intrigued me. I met with the museum leadership and began the conversation. I learned it was going to be quite the lift, but the impact it could bring to the community was going to be worth the effort. Not familiar with the process of curating an exhibit, I leaned on them for the process and reached out to other Black leaders in the community to gather ideas on what should be displayed. After several meetings with the museum leadership and the community, I felt we had enough ideas and a process, but the most challenging part was raising the funds. Fortunately, many people loved this vision, so when I was able to have someone take over the chamber, she had a network that would be able to carry this project forward. And being a full-time leader for the chamber with her level of experience, the process and fundraising became a lot easier, and we see the museum coming to fruition in 2024. The purpose of the museum is to educate the community on the Black experience. Our nation has become so polarized that it has been challenging to form common ground. The museum could be that bridge to connect and engage the community. I'm always trying to look for opportunities to build an environment for us to better understand one another.

THE BLACK CHAMBER FOUNDATION AND BLACK SUCCESS CENTER

The pandemic and the social justice movement of 2020 shed light on the many disparities in the Black community. While I felt the chamber was a solution to some of the economic disparities, there were still gaps in the community that weren't being filled. The "revolving door" of professionals of color was still a challenge. While Living Color Utah, its organizations, and the community were still working hard on their mission, the Black community was still losing top talent, and the negative narrative of Black Utah was still prevalent. In social events I attended, I often heard people talking about how they planned to relocate out of state. What really got to me was hearing from a few that had children. They didn't want their kids going through the public school system, or they had kids experiencing racism and bullying in school, and nothing was being done about it. The growth of remote work also provided more opportunities for these families to relocate sooner without needing to look for another company to work for. This was unacceptable to me. I've worked too hard for this community to still hear about these challenges. It was almost a shot to me saying, "James, you're not doing enough." I took it personally.

I though, what if we could create a hub for the community? The great thing about Utah is we are so integrated. While redlining was prevalent in the early 1900s, it didn't impact Utah as much as in other states. While there are a few cities that have a lot of diversity, we are all spread out for the most part. The downside of that, however, is that it makes it challenging for new residents to find Utah's diversity. The vision is that we could curate a space where people can come and get connected to Utah's Black community at any time and learn about resources, attend events, and grow their businesses. Something like a coworking space with a community center intertwined. That was the inspiration behind the Black Success Center. The chamber's nonprofit was already focused on programming, and the Black Success Center could be the home of that programming and the Black Chamber. Once again, I was trying to build a concept I didn't know how to build, but since when did that ever stop me? I leaned on some people that I had met over the years to help me develop this concept. I met a Black developer from the east coast a few years ago. He was visiting Salt Lake City as a potential opportunity to develop housing. I reached out to him to see if he could give me some direction on how to go about finding funding and building this facility. His thought was to put affordable housing around it, which would almost guarantee funding from banks through their community reinvestment department. I never considered housing as an opportunity for me and my organizations, but it was worth a shot. I thought a financial literacy program would complement something like this to help people transition from affordable housing to homeownership and housing that program in the Black Success Center. The developer put together some designs of what it would look like and I got really excited. This could really happen. So, I started moving on it.

I wrote down plans for an incubator program for small businesses, classroom training to develop professionals, and community events. I felt this was going to be an epic hub for our community. I started working on a budget and a plan for funding. When I started to encounter barriers on how to move forward on this, I reached out to the developer. Each time, he became slower and slower to respond, and then he just stopped responding. I never heard back from him again. Once again, I was too deep into this process and passionate about it to stop moving, so I began reaching out to my network for support. Everyone I spoke to loved the concept. However, I was still "ignorance on fire," but that was better than "knowledge on ice." I met with a realtor and a bank and found a building, and I was going to have to raise $4 million dollars in five months. Somehow, I thought that was doable, and everyone else did, too. I mean, I've accomplished so much already that there wasn't much doubt that I could do this, too. But this time, my ignorance defeated my passion. I fell severely short of raising the funds. I wasn't even close. However, we developed a relationship with a new co-working space being developed downtown, and they loved the idea of us partnering together to run the Black Success Center out of their space. We still have a vision of our own space and are still in that process. In the meantime, we are grateful for the relationships we have to move the programming forward while we work through the process of having our own building.

A PATH FOR THE FUTURE

The youth was still a challenge I hadn't yet tackled. While hearing about the youth experiencing challenges in the public school system, I wasn't sure if this was my lane. However, if Black professionals were leaving Utah, I felt I had to figure out how I could support them with a solution. Someone must have read my mind because last year, I was approached by another organization that was working with a high school on a career and college readiness program. They invited me to join their team as a community partner. It took several meetings and business convenings for me to figure out how I could be the best partner for them, but then it started clicking. I recalled the conversations I was hearing about families wanting to leave Utah. Students were having these conversations as well. As soon as they graduated high school, their hope, just like my friends when I was in high school, was to leave Utah. College students had this mindset as well. The community has grown, and many didn't have the village I grew up with. I knew that if they were introduced to that same or similar village, they would probably stay.

A friend of mine from Cincinnati had this event called Men of Promise. He and I had always talked about bringing this event to Utah. I reached out to him, and we designed the plan to make it happen. In October of 2022, we hosted over 250 high school boys, most of them boys of color, in a large corporate facility and shared with them how to believe in their dreams. We had male professionals from around the community sit at the tables with these boys and mentor them and talk to them. This is what we needed. The Men of Promise Conference was a huge hit. A few of the school district leaders loved the event and plan to invite more students to the next one. I also started putting together career fairs for high school students and programming to support their path to getting internships or starting their careers. I spoke with companies to host students to take them on a tour of their facility and share what opportunities are there for them and even ask their employees if they would welcome some job shadowing. The goal is to build a bridge between corporate and schools so these students have a better understanding of what is out there for them. I don't want them to leave Utah because they believe there is nothing here for them. If they leave, it will be because they had the choice of opportunities here or somewhere else, and they chose that opportunity somewhere else was better for them. I know we won't be able to keep every student in Utah, but if we make that the goal, they'll see that we care about them and their future. They'll see that there is a village of support surrounding them.

CAPACITY > PASSION

I am on a mission, but I am only one person. Over the last couple of years, I realized that my passion is far exceeding my capacity to accomplish everything. People began to introduce me as "James Jackson, founder of the Utah Black Chamber, who does so many other things." Over time, it began to kind of get to me. I was so focused on my purpose that I never paid attention to my own brand. I had my hand involved in nearly anything that focused on growing this community. But how do I want to represent myself? How could I accomplish everything without losing my mind?

REFLECTION

Sometimes your passion can push you beyond your own capacity. This is why it's important to build leaders in the process. Think about the team you have around you – family, friends, community. How can they support you? Don't allow yourself to stop just because you can't give anymore. That just means you have big dreams.

INFLUENCE: THE NEXT EPISODE

THE GROWTH of the chamber and other projects became overwhelming. I could not keep up with it and feared a catastrophe if something didn't change. Systems that were set up were operating at an efficient level, with me overseeing the operations, but that was all I was able to focus on. My voice was consistently being requested elsewhere; panel discussions, local commercials and ads, board and committee meetings, my full-time job, and most importantly, my family. There was no balance, and something was going to have to give. I looked at the chamber's budget and decided that it was time. While still a little nervous about the next step, there was really no other choice. The vision I had for the chamber was far beyond my experience and capacity. It was time for a new leader.

SUCCESSION

At our September 2021 board retreat, the Utah Black Chamber board of directors developed and approved the job description and posting for a president & CEO. Upon reviewing the job description, I asked them, "Was I doing *all* of that?" It was no wonder I was about to go crazy! This organization that started to support a small Black community in the state of Utah had grown to become one of the most influential diverse organizations in the state, supporting a growing and thriving community. This next step was not only necessary, but the community depended on it. My only concern was, where would we find this person? In the beginning, not many people in our community even knew what a chamber of commerce was, and now we are looking for someone to lead it. We would have to do a national search. I didn't know how that was going to work, but we had to figure it out.

The search took several months. Most of the candidates were local, with only a couple from out of state. Both of the out-of-state candidates were familiar with Utah and used to live here. I had my eye on one candidate already. She was local and was very familiar with the community and many of the small Black businesses. With a little mentoring on how a chamber of commerce works, I felt she would do fine. In reality, this was me settling. I was already in the mindset of not being able to find someone to carry my vision forward. I was prepared to give myself a year with the new leader to train and mentor them. The board interviewed my preferred candidate, had the same feelings as me, and began discussing the offer. However, the book, *Black Utah*, was about to be released, and we were doing some social media promotion around it. The book caught the eye of an individual familiar with Utah and heard about the chamber from mutual connections. She was impressed with the concept of the book and did more research about the Black Chamber. In her research, she discovered the job posting. We connected on LinkedIn, and she asked if this posting was true. I answered yes and asked if she was interested. I didn't even know who Dr. Sidni Lloyd-Shorter was. I hadn't yet looked at her profile when I asked if she was interested. That was the desperation in me. Sidni thought about it. She wasn't looking for a job. She owned a successful business. After some consideration, though, she followed up with me, and we chatted about the position. All I could think to myself was, "God loves me." I wanted to do everything we possibly could to hire her. I called one of my board members and asked to hold off on the offer to the other candidate and set up a time to talk to Sidni. The board was just as impressed. Her experience, eloquence, charisma, background, and expertise were a Godsend. We knew she would do amazing work, and we figured out how to bring her to Utah from Baton Rouge, Louisiana, to become the new president & CEO of the Utah Black Chamber.

Sidni began her role in April 2022. As we approach a year with her at the helm at the time of writing this book, she has grown the chamber another 130%, expanded our platform beyond Utah borders, hosted several events, and established a partnership with the National Basketball Association for NBA All-Star weekend. She implemented programs for small businesses, and our First Fridays attendance has had the most amazing energy. Black businesses have become more visible, and she has provided more opportunities for them in different events throughout the community. Sidni also received many individual accolades as well, using her platform and influence to grow our community. A month before her one-year anniversary as the Black Chamber CEO, she was honored by Utah Business Magazine as one of their CEOs of the year and made the cover! While I was prepared to have to train and mentor our new leader, my main role in supporting Sidni was simply getting her connected. She began hiring staff to support her, and I have been assisting in training them, while I continue to witness my vision continue moving forward.

DEEP FOR DOUGH VS. WIDE FOR SHOW

In network marketing, one of the most important things to learn is the compensation plan. It's the compensation plan that guides you on how to build your business. Structured the wrong way, you can potentially miss out on production and income. There are so many different types of compensation structures within the industry, and they all fall under three main structures – binary, uni-level, and matrix. When you begin building your team, the goal is to structure your team to maximize your income. Built one way, you can earn a lot of money upfront, or in another way, you can earn a little income consistently over time. In the network marketing business I was in, the compensation structure was set up to earn a lot of income by recruiting people directly to your front line, so they were placed directly under you. You can build as wide as you like. The challenge is that there is more leadership responsibility that is needed on those direct recruits by mentoring them and helping them close sales. If you go too wide, you may lose people, particularly those who rely more on your mentorship and leadership. Alternatively, suppose you can meet a certain production level. In that case, you can earn that similar income by only building so wide directly under you, and then anyone else that joins your team, you can strategically place them in those business lines or teams to help build others. If you can strengthen other teams well enough, you have the potential to earn a strong passive income with less effort coming from you. This allows you to identify strong leaders within the team to work with, mentor them, guide them, and help build a team around them to support their growth.

These concepts can also be applied to your purpose. Many set out to build an organization but set their vision within their own limited capabilities. They build as many relationships as possible that can support their efforts and try to be the go-to person to as many of them as they can. This will only work for so long before success reaches a peak or the person begins to burn out. Over time the flame dies down with some people, and those who maintain the flame are only given so much energy from their leader. I see this happen with many people. They feel the way to becoming a great leader is by knowing a lot of people. Growing everyone is not sustainable. To build the legacy I want to build, I knew I had to identify some key individuals who could carry my vision forward or had a vision aligned with my purpose. I keep those individuals close, and I work to surround them with influencers and resources and provide guidance and mentorship when they need it. Some of these individuals may or may not know that I have them as part of the core team. I don't announce it or proclaim it to the world. Of course, for someone like Sidni, it's automatic. She took over my baby, the Utah Black Chamber, so I am going to make sure she has everything she needs to succeed. When you have someone like Sidni, they, too, are building their team, and if there's someone I feel would connect better with her than I, I'll make an introduction and allow the connection to happen organically. "Deep for dough" is the best route for me. I don't have the capacity or energy to be a popular, go-to kind of person. I am not interested in being everywhere all the time. But I am someone that can elevate someone's vision. I want them to win, and I want to cheer them on and provide whatever resource or contact to help them thrive.

LEAD TO LEAD LEADERS

Witnessing the growth of the Chamber, I felt the urge inside of me to begin replacing myself in every role I have been committed to. Sidni's success showed me how attractive and inspiring my vision is. All I needed to do was find the right people to lead out on it. How much could be accomplished if I had someone like Sidni in all my other roles? I began to embrace who I was as a leader in this community. I had to remind myself that it was me who attracted Sidni Shorter, and it was time to use that influence to identify and attract more leaders. Since then, I have developed a strong core leadership team.

I have known Deonn Henderson for a while. He was the CEO of Miss Essie's BBQ, a company led by one of my friends, Marcus Jones. I've known Marcus since college and have watched him grow his business for the last 20 years. Deonn and Marcus were high school friends in Arizona, and Deonn has been working in the Washington, DC, area as an entrepreneur and investor. While trying to figure out the Black Success Center, one of my board members strongly encouraged me to talk to Deonn. I knew Deonn traveled back and forth from DC to Salt Lake for business, but at the time, I didn't fully know his role with Miss Essie's. He also started one of the most successful Black incubators in the country, the Startup Nest. When he and I connected, and he began sharing what he did with the Startup Nest, I was stunned. This is why that board member strongly encouraged me to speak with him! He already had the vision of the Black Success Center built out. Between Deonn and Sidni, my two biggest projects have strong leaders who share my desire to make an impact. My main focus now is to ensure that I guide them to the right influencers and supporting organizations, provide the perspective of being a native of this state, share my understanding of the cadence, culture, and capabilities. I'm so grateful they share the same passion as me and together, and I'm excited for what we are about to accomplish.

My support staff from the foundation has been incredible as well. Elle Solomon has been by my side since 2014. Her background is in nonprofit law, and she has made sure we had all our compliance and legal requirements in order for the three entities. She left for the east coast to earn her doctorate degree and came back to the organization last year to work for the foundation to help build out our programming in addition to what she was already doing. Elle has always believed in me since the beginning. She was amazed at my vision and bought into seeing it through. Whenever I feel like I need a pep talk or a confidence booster, Elle is there, either intentionally or unintentionally. I am always encouraged and motivated after a chat with her. I believe everyone needs an Elle Solomon. Someone who simply works in the background to make sure all your ducks are in order while encouraging you to push through.

Cameron Williams' family established the Cameron Russell Williams Impact Fund to continue Cameron's legacy. Part of that fund is working with the University of Utah to provide scholarships to students who want to work in tech and/or are new entrepreneurs. The first recipient of that scholarship was Daisy Hall. Daisy was a freshman and had her own business as well. Meeting with her briefly, I could tell she was pretty sharp. Daisy was a native of Utah as well, raised in Ogden. The CRW Impact Fund committee and Daisy attended a luncheon held by the University of Utah, and in conversation, Daisy mentioned that she was open to an internship in the summer. My ears perked up, and I immediately met with her. It was a no-brainer for me, and she was excited to join the team. I didn't fully know her capabilities, but I was going to learn quickly. We had so much movement going on in the foundation, with programs still in their infant stage, so I had very little time to train someone. My hope was that I could share what we needed to be done and that she had the experience to do it without little oversight from me or anyone else. Daisy was not only equipped with the experience we needed, but she was a visionary as well. She saw what we were trying to do and was excited about our mission. I no longer see Daisy as an intern but part of the leadership team. We have weekly calls to discuss our projects and ideas, and Daisy leads a lot of our community efforts, contacts businesses to help them find resources, contacts new entrepreneurs to enroll them in our programs, manages our social media, and leads our events. This past year, I had her lead our Evening in Harlem event, and she did an extraordinary job. I put myself in a supportive role for her and empowered her to lead. I wanted to see how far she can go as a leader, and she continues to succeed.

"If you want to fast, go alone. If you want to go far, go together."

– AFRICAN PROVERB

A combination of being tired and excited to see more leaders aligned with my vision showed me that I don't always have to be in front. My strength has always been as a servant leader. I love the opportunity to support others, and now I have a significantly larger platform than when I started to support someone at any level, whether they are just starting out and I can mentor them, or they are a CEO, and I can be a connector. Contributing to someone's success has become addictive for me. If I believe in your purpose, I'm always thinking about how I can help you. I recall listening to Steve Harvey's story, and he shared how he wanted to become the "Nike Swoosh" of entertainment. Nike started out as just shoes, and now they have apparel and sports equipment. Nike is everywhere when it comes to sports, and Steve wanted to be that for entertainment. In the beginning, I wanted to do the same thing for my community. I wanted to have my hands in everything and be the solution to all of our community's problems. But I realized it doesn't work for me that way. The best way is to identify strong leaders and use my platform for support. The more leaders I can find to take on my current initiatives, the more available I can be for others.

MENTORS MAGNIFY, ALLIES AMPLIFY

Mentors and allies are the main reasons for the chamber's success. The Hispanic Chamber was with me at the beginning, providing guidance and knowledge on how to grow the chamber. My grandfather introduced me to a talent I didn't know I possessed. From there, he provided a path for me to grow, and all I had to do was continue following that path. I am thankful for all the mentors who have provided me with their wisdom and guidance to help me and the chamber grow. They helped magnify my talents and abilities to me and to the community, and I continue to walk down the path to growth. It's important we all have mentors in our lives. We should never try to navigate this world alone. We are all equipped with the potential to succeed, and we just need the right influence around us to open our eyes and guide us down the right path. My goal now is to pay this mentorship forward, either directly or indirectly. I felt I had so much on my plate that I wouldn't be able to give the time necessary to mentor someone. However, people have shared with me that I have been mentoring this whole time. They watched my work, heard me speak at an event or simply just followed me on social media. People who want to be mentored will seek out any opportunity to get guidance from those they admire. I have done the same with national speakers and authors. I read their books, listen to their podcasts, or attend their events. Mentorship is not a large task. It can be as simple as talking to someone for just a couple of minutes and sharing your experience. Mainly, just being an example is mentorship. My hope is this book lays a foundation to serve as a mentor to many.

I was speaking on a diversity and inclusion panel, and the topic of allies was being discussed. During our conversation, I began to think about how allies support the BIPOC (Black, Indigenous, and People of Color). Allies elevate the voices of those underrepresented or unheard. Allies can help get a message to people for them when they can't, to support a cause, advocate, or open a door of opportunity that has been traditionally closed for them. Since the beginning of the chamber, I attribute a lot of our success to the allies we have developed relationships with. Not only have they helped amplify our voice, but they have also been mentors and listeners. Allies are just as important as mentors. While the social justice movement has focused on allies for underrepresented communities, organizations like the Black Chamber and influencers like myself can also be allies.

People are creating opportunities all the time, but they just need a little boost of confidence, guidance, and a voice larger than theirs. We are all equipped with a certain level of influence, gifts, and abilities. They are given to us for a purpose, and part of that purpose is to share who we are with others to elevate them. It is in our nature to serve others. Imagine if we all just took a little time out of our schedule to be a mentor or ally to someone. It could be that one piece of advice or that one door that you helped open for them that can change their whole trajectory.

REFLECTION

A legacy doesn't have to be about the success of a business or organization. It doesn't have to be an idea. A legacy is simply your purpose living beyond you. How do you ensure your purpose continues long after you leave this earth? How have your mentors provided a path for you, and how can you do that for others? Do you have allies? Who can you reach out to for allyship? Your plan doesn't have to end with you. If you have a big vision and are passionate about your purpose, people will come from all over for support. I'm thankful for my grandfather helping me find my purpose, and I am continually inspired by his legacy.

15

ENDURANCE: TAKE CARE OF YOU

"Self-control is strength. Calmness is mastery. You have to get to a point where your mood doesn't shift based on the insignificant actions of someone else. Don't allow others to control the direction of your life. Don't allow your emotions to overpower your intelligence."

– MORGAN FREEMAN

MAY 25, 2020 was a hard day for the Black community. It wasn't the fact it was something we hadn't seen before. The media shared two other reports earlier in the year of similar incidents. This was different. We are all at home in quarantine from the COVID-19 pandemic, and the nine-minute video showing the murder of George Floyd was all over the media. Most of the country witnessed what the Black community has witnessed since we arrived on this land. I watched that video more than once, which was one too many. I first saw it when my friend sent it to me via text, asking if I had seen it. He couldn't believe it. He was so upset. It didn't hit me at first. Maybe because I was numb to it, sad to say. His feelings caused me to check my emotions. Should I be more upset? Why wasn't I as upset as he was?

Growing up, I rarely showed my emotions. I was always quiet and reserved. Rarely have people ever seen me angry. Even today, I rarely show my anger. People may have seen me frustrated, sad, or anxious, but not angry. My dad had a temper. He's gotten a lot better, but growing up, his temper was embarrassing to me. When we were out golfing, and he hit a bad shot, he would throw his club and yell. For a while, I tried to avoid playing with him. I believe that from seeing his anger, I went the total opposite route. I don't allow things to get to me. As I have developed in my leadership, I have found that there is a solution to every problem, and I will be more effective identifying the solution if I stay calm. Anger is a response to a cause, and I was taught that life is 10% what happens to you and 90% how you respond. If I hit a bad shot on the golf course, I think about why I am out golfing in the first place. I'm out there to enjoy the outdoors and play a game I love while taking a moment to get away from the grind in life. Golf, for me, is a relaxing time. I can't get angry during a time when I'm supposed to be relaxing. Of course, I don't want to hit a bad shot, but I know my skill level, and I do want to be better. Playing better will take time, and I have to respect the process. If I want to play better, I have to play more often. The few times I do get angry is when something I should be able to control and I no longer can. For example, several years ago, Michelle and I went out for drinks with friends, and my sister and her friends joined us. Unfortunately, one of her friends had a little too much to drink. People act in certain ways when they get inebriated. For her, she talked nonstop. We were trying to take her home, but she talked so much, we had a hard time getting the opportunity to ask her for directions to her house! The half-hour drive to her house was all about listening to her. It didn't matter what we tried to say or chime in. It drove me crazy. She was getting to all of us. I could not wait until she was out of the car. I had visions of dropping her off on the side of the road! I allowed her to get to my emotions, and this was Michelle's first time seeing me angry. We had been dating for about two years at the time. I was quiet, and I tightly clenched the steering wheel with an intense scowl facing the road. Michelle had never seen that look on my face.

May 2020 was a different set of emotions. Being stuck at home for a couple of months, our family wanted to get out of the house, so we took a hiking trip to southern Utah. I began seeing and reading about protests and riots across the country, and one evening in our hotel room, I witnessed these protests and riots happening in my own hometown – a place that doesn't have that much diversity. The chamber leadership contacted me, asking what our next step should be. Leaders throughout the community also reached out, asking how they could help and become a stronger allies. The overwhelming feeling of seeing the racial injustice, along with the outpouring of support and ally-ship, was too much. At the peak of one of our hikes the next day, I just broke down crying. It just happened out of nowhere. I wasn't ready. Michelle and our daughter, Zoe, weren't ready either. As a calm and laid-back person, emotions don't come out of me a lot. But there was no holding back. It wasn't that I didn't know what to do. It wasn't that I couldn't handle it. I didn't want to hide from it all. I. Needed. To. Let. Go. The dam of everything that was pent up inside of me, naturally just being strong for my family and my community, just broke. Hearing and seeing people revealing their true selves of being prejudiced and bigoted over the last few years was hard enough, but it continued to bring opportunities to educate and elevate the importance of a diversity, equity, and inclusion strategy in government, corporate, and community. But even that hit its peak at this moment.

Over the next several months, the chamber experienced hyper-growth. People and companies were joining the chamber nearly every day. Our leadership and board grew. We developed new programming. On the other end, however, the media took a bigger turn for the worse. There were constant debates and fighting online regarding people's views about our country. I got sucked in at times. I tried so hard not to respond, but with some of the ignorance I saw, I felt that I could bring some enlightenment in the way I communicate, but it still didn't work. That summer was one of the most emotional experiences of my life. Those breaking-down moments happened several times over the summer. Often, it occurred while sitting alone after dinner or after work. Sometimes, Michelle or one of the kids would come to console me. Other times, they felt I'd be better if I was left alone to have the release I needed. I spent many evenings on the back patio reflecting on things or having conversations with Michelle. My comfort zone was forced to be stretched and be more engaged in the community as not only an advocate but an activist. I was called to lead, facilitate, and moderate discussions and panels on diversity, equity, and inclusion. I have never considered myself a practitioner of diversity, equity, and inclusion, but my voice and influence were more important, and I called on my DEI practitioner friends to mentor and partner with me. The year 2020 was the most challenging and exhausting year of my life. However, my leadership elevated significantly, and I learned a lot about my mental endurance and how my emotions can impact my influence.

LISTENING FOR WHAT THEY WANT TO HEAR

We have so many ways to use our voice nowadays, and our words can have a greater impact than ever before. And unfortunately, it's a negative impact we hear more. Entertainers and influencers have lost followers, contracts, and endorsements and have even been outright "canceled" because of something they posted online or said in an interview. Local leaders can be impacted by this as well. With all these channels to use our voice, we have to understand that someone is always listening. Sometimes people will come with an ear that hears words differently, coming from a different perspective. Others are on a mission to criticize. Leaders will always have haters, and the "bigger the level, the bigger the devil." Growing up, I thought leaders had to be the outgoing, sociable type of individual. But leadership is not always about speaking. It's about knowing the right time to speak and how to effectively communicate your message in as few words as possible. I was taught to have a core group of friends, family, or team with a strong connection and trust to allow myself to vent and express my full emotion. Venting to the world does not serve you well in most cases. The more you share, the less control you have over your voice. As I mentioned, people are going to come with their own ears and hear what they want to hear, so even saying less isn't always going to work, but at least you have more control and can expound on your message if needed.

I've learned to stay out of battles that don't serve me or my purpose. I realize we want to try to educate or correct someone, but with a nation so divided, it's important to choose where your voice will impact most. This could be writing a letter to your state and federal legislators, having conversations with city and county policymakers, meeting with your boss and/or your boss's boss, or just having a community conversation. I watched a TED Talk given by Theo EJ Wilson. He shared his journey of going undercover on social media as Lucious25, a white supremacist lurker, so he could gain perspective from those that thought differently from him. What he found was an unexpected compassion and surprising perspective when engaging with people he disagreed with. In his talk, he encourages us to embrace curiosity and have courageous conversations in order to build bridges. From this experiment, he began having these "courageous conversations" in barbershops and salons. He became the executive director of Shop Talk Live, which hosts bimonthly gatherings in select barber shops in Colorado. They're open to anyone and frequently focus on issues affecting the Black community. These gatherings are also streamed on social media, gaining thousands of views. Choose your battles wisely. But also, go where you can make the most impact for change.

CAPACITY VS. CLARITY

I'm a visionary. I identify opportunities for change and love to engage with those who can help make it happen, or I create on my own. When ideas come, I put them in my Google Drive. I am able to deliver a training or a talk on the fly, because I already have them developed. The saying "if you stay ready, you never have to get ready" is part of my MO. The Utah Black Chamber was never a plan of mine in the beginning, but as it grew and it evolved, I saw where we could make the most impact and worked toward that. Because of that, it has become one of the most diverse and fastest-growing chambers of commerce in the state of Utah. It's definitely not because of the size of our community but rather, the size of the vision. The stronger your purpose is, the less quantity matters. However, there does come a point where your vision begins to become blurry, ideas are not coming like you want them, and you feel on the brink, just going through the motions. That's where I found myself over the last two years.

I was on several boards and committees, and I was in the process of developing a couple more organizations and projects in addition to leading the chamber, its nonprofit, *and* having a full-time job. My own business, J3 Motivation, took a bit of a back seat. I was giving fewer talks and not doing any training or masterminds. The chamber's growth accelerated significantly in 2020, and I was called to be out in the community more than I ever have. I knew it was good for the chamber and for myself to have that type of exposure, and it opened my eyes to how much influence I had gained over the last several years. However, I became tired faster, and I found myself getting lazy and more reactive. I knew something had to change. I did some reflecting on why I was so tired and why I wasn't able to create like I used to. Then it dawned on me. I was at an event, and someone I worked with in the community wanted to introduce me to someone she thought I should get to know. "Meet James Jackson, III. He is the founder of the Utah Black Chamber and does a million other things." I think I may have heard an introduction like this before, but at that moment, it hit differently. Did I want to be known as the guy that does a million things? Is that a good thing? Obviously, not at that moment, because I realized why I was so tired and my brain wasn't working like it used to.

People always ask how I do it all. I do it all because of my passion and my work ethic. I've always put my head down and grinded. I have never looked for fame or fortune. I read a quote that said, "Hustle in silence and let your success make all the noise." I know my hustle. Well, I thought I did until my hustle met its match. I met my capacity. As I reflected on that introduction and what it said about me, I began hearing it more and more. This is how people know me. I began to silently dislike this introduction. I continued to allow people to introduce me that way, and it continued to serve as a reminder to me that things had to change. I began seeing how my mental capacity began to affect my home and my overall mental state. I was not mentally well, and I didn't even realize it. I was so much into my grind that I didn't take the time to check in with myself. I didn't allow my family to check in with me. Michelle was giving me several warnings about how I was off my game, and I was in denial that I wasn't. I was overly consumed in all I was doing. I didn't know I was off. I didn't feel I was off. Whenever I was working on a project or an event, Michelle would ask, "Is this for the chamber, nonprofit, J3, or Zions?" In conversations with others, she would comment on how exhausting it was for her to support me. I couldn't see it. If my biggest supporter, cheerleader, confidant, and partner in life can't keep up, how can she support me? How do I expect her to keep up if I am having a hard time keeping up with myself? After Sidni was brought in to lead the chamber and my role began to diminish, things became clearer. I began meeting with a mental health coach and a therapist to help give me some clarity. I wanted to get back to visionary status again.

What I realized is that I had allowed myself to get away from me. It took some time to figure it out, but I realized that I had allowed myself to be defined by my positions and not my purpose. That's what people saw– all the organizations and projects that I created and led, books I have written, talks I have given–everything was isolated, and I didn't do a good job sharing my overall vision and purpose. For me to do that, for me to get back to visionary status, I needed to let go. Ego has never played a role in my life. My success has been how I impact the success of others. It allows me to stay in the background and stick to my purpose. For the last two years, I have been out front and center. Moving on from the chamber was the first step. I also began stepping down from boards and committees that didn't mutually benefit or align with my purpose. Most importantly, I began identifying people who I could pass on the torch. I either passed the torch directly, like Dr. Sidni Shorter becoming the new president & CEO of the chamber, or I handed it off more subtly where I positioned others to lead in areas where I felt I needed to step away. Over time, I began gaining back clarity. It wasn't until the end of 2022 that I found it, but I'm so grateful I did. I've found my way back to living with purpose.

Your mental capacity determines your ability to take on tasks based on your skills, experience, and talent. Your clarity is more purposeful. It involves the heart and how you want to leverage your capacity to make the impact you desire. You can continue grinding, but you can get to a point where your brain says it can't take anymore. It won't shut down, but it will struggle to navigate the path you created, and you will lose focus on who you are and what you desire to become. It's a dopamine effect. Dopamine is a chemical released in your brain that makes you feel good. Having the right amount of dopamine is good for your body and your brain. The challenge is understanding the right activities that affect your dopamine. There are many things out there that make you feel good: accomplishments, compliments, good food, movies, sports, sex, I could go on. However, there are other things that make you feel good that are not necessarily good like drugs and alcohol. This is how addictions are formed, because of that need to "feel good." So while you're feeling good about all that you're accomplishing, once that "high" comes down, it can lead to being tired, moody, unmotivated, or even depressed. The key is finding clarity. Once you find clarity, you can keep your dopamine levels at a healthy state for your well-being. Clarity helps you find focus and direction for your life. Your work life and home life must be in harmony with each other. When you have clarity around your goals and priorities, it's easier to move towards what you want out of life.

A BLACK TAX

As a Black man, more specifically, a Black man in Utah, I put a lot on my shoulders. I carry a lot of unnecessary burdens I've been given living in this country. Because of that, I, as well as many Black men, tend to hold on to our feelings a lot. I want to show my strength to everyone and never any of my weaknesses. I want to show my "Superman" mentality all the time. I know I can do it all. I can take on the world and whatever is stacked against me and conquer it. But what the pandemic period revealed to me is that it's okay not to be okay at times. I can't be Superman all the time. Even Superman had kryptonite. I now understand fully that I can't be everything to everyone at all times. But I do have to be everything to myself. I have to be true to myself. I have to be real with myself. Growing up in Utah and being surrounded by the village my parents provided for me, I understood that I not only represent myself in the world, I represent my family, my church, the company I work for, and a Black man. I have to defeat the stereotypes a Black man carries, the judgments against us, and the perception of what we are capable of.

"Don't forget what I am. Don't forget who I am. I am a black dude. And don't forget how I got here. My ancestors were kidnapped, I don't even know where the fuck I'm from. They were put on the bottom of boats. They sailed across the Atlantic. Many of them died. Only the strongest survived. And once they got here, they beat the humanity out of my people. They turned us into beasts of burden. They made us do their work, and the irony is hundreds of years later, they're calling us lazy. We fought in the civil war, we damn near freed ourselves. Now we are all here. Four hundred year nightmare. Took us four hundred years to figure out as a people. The white people's weakness the whole time. Was kneeling during the national anthem."

—DAVE CHAPELLE

Former Utah Jazz player Donovan Mitchell shared in an interview that it was draining for him trying to do good in Utah as not only a Black man but as a Black man with a platform. I can only imagine how draining it was for him with his status compared to what I am feeling at a much smaller level. As much as I try to do good in the world, it does get draining, and it's important that I check in with myself. It's important to take time for myself. I began unplugging the last two weeks of the year a couple of years ago. When I'm on vacation, I'm. On. Vacation. I fully check out. I trust my team will handle business, and I allow myself to be on vacation to fully rest and recover. I grind so hard throughout the year that I need time to recharge. With all that I was pouring into my work, it wasn't enough. I overdid it and needed to find a way to pull back. As I have grown older and grown my influence, I know things have to change for me to keep growing forward. Accomplishing all that I want to accomplish doesn't mean working harder. It's not about just working smarter. It's about identifying my limits and finding a path that keeps me grounded and clear. "God will only give me what I can handle. I just wish he didn't trust me so much."

These last two years helped me understand what God put me here to do. Nothing more, nothing less. If I do too much, I'm overwhelmed and don't feel well. If I do less, then I'm unmotivated and uninspired. It's okay to admit when you're not okay. Whether it be to a mental health coach, a therapist, family, or close ones, you need that outlet, especially we Black men. To continue to be as strong as we want to be, we have to be human and allow people to come into our lives to help lift us up when we need help and not try to lift ourselves up all the time. Over time, you won't be able to lift yourself up. We've seen so many people over the last couple of years put an end to their life because they couldn't get out of the darkness they were in. Life is not easy. Nothing rewarding, nothing worthwhile, nothing worth having, is going to be easy. It's going to be hard. Life is going to test you. Life isn't fair, and it's not supposed to be. We were all placed here to accomplish something, and it can't be accomplished if everything is fair. Having a mental health coach and a therapist has provided me with the conversations I needed to give me back the clarity I once had.

THE POWER OF MY FAITH

"I think everybody has a purpose. Everybody is made to be a picture of how good and glorious God is, and I think sometimes we'll get it confused and think because we mess up, we make mistakes or we have some blemishes in our record, that our purpose is somehow messed up. But actually that only serves to further paint a picture of how good God is when he uses people who are messed up just like me."[1]

— LECRAE

Faith in a higher power puts power behind my purpose. I believe we are all here for a reason. We are all given special gifts and talents and positioned in certain areas. I share with people often that I would not have been able to accomplish what I accomplished in Utah in any other state in the amount of time I have had. I was in the right culture and circumstances, in combination with my influences, education, experience, gifts, and talents. It was impossible to void my purpose in life. The good, bad, and ugly about life groomed me, strengthened me, and educated me.

"For I am not ashamed of the gospel, because it is the power of God that brings salvation to everyone who believes."

— ROMANS 1:16

Born and raised with religion, it's difficult for me to imagine how life would be without it. I am not trying to push religion on anyone. I'm only sharing my lived experiences, and I feel it's important to believe in a higher power than what is available on this earth. Whether it's a religion, the universe, or something all-powerful you can call one when times are tough. Gospel artist Kirk Franklin said, "God may allow us to hit rock bottom to show us He's the rock at the bottom." I have had many experiences where I had nowhere else to turn or had an unexpected blessing come my way that I only can see my belief in God as my answer. Belief in God was my first step in reading personal development books.

A GROWTH PLAN

I began reading books on personal growth shortly after college. It was the most important thing network marketing introduced me to. I never knew about personal growth. I thought my education stopped when I finished school. Network marketing introduced me to the concept of continual learning.

Personal development changed my life. I consider myself a NERD – Never Ending Research and Development. I haven't read a lot of books. I admit I'm a slow reader, and I don't go for the amount of books I can read. My focus is to read books that apply to where I am trying to grow next and what I am trying to accomplish. I may have read books more than once, or I stopped reading a book before finishing it because it no longer applied to me or I didn't align with its vision. When I read a book, I want to make sure I am able to apply what I learned.

When I started my J3 business, I developed a personal growth plan. Nothing formal, but more of a commitment. A commitment to reading, writing, listening, applying, and teaching. I read to learn. I am always seeking ways that I can become a better person. I write down all the ideas that come to my head, whether it's a training, a blog piece, a potential article, training or even a book. Although I am a horrible note-taker, I spend hours in front of a computer writing out a thought in my head. I listen to podcasts, audiobooks, interviews, or sometimes documentaries. I used to just focus on self-improvement material, but I realized in order for me to become a better person, I have to be more well-rounded and keep updated on what's going on in the world around me and discover other interests I may want to pursue in the future. I can't be a business person all the time.

For me to retain everything that I'm reading and listening to, writing can't be my only outlet to retain the information. I have to be able to apply as well. That's the only way I'm going to be able to grow. The Utah Black Chamber has become my personal growth journey. Prior to founding the organization, I was fine with a corporate job, working my way up to the top and just dealing with whatever life handed to me. The network marketing business opened my mind, and I realized how much more this world offers. The chamber helped me become the person I am today by realizing my purpose and working on my passion. My gift now is sharing with others what I learned as I hope to inspire others to take their journey of finding their purpose. After all, that's why we are here – to live with purpose.

REFLECTION

The pathway to growth is not easy, and over the last few years, just living hasn't been easy for many of us. If you haven't made time to check in with yourself, I encourage you to do so now. No matter how strong you may think you are or think you feel, life will throw challenges your way to test that strength. Don't feel you have to push through. Sometimes the results won't outweigh the consequences. Sometimes you have to slow down to speed up. Sometimes, you just have to pause and reflect. Sometimes, you may just have to stop and reverse course. Take a few minutes now and think about how you are feeling right now. What's causing you stress, pain, anxiety, or worry? What methods should you consider for healing?

PART FIVE
CONCLUSION

16
CONCLUSION

Passion. Influence. Endurance. This is how I live with purpose every single day.

I AM A COMMUNITY BUILDER. I discovered this purpose by discovering my passion for speaking and using that ability to connect and elevate people. The Black Chamber was the vehicle that helped me grow my influence and become the person I needed to be to live out my purpose. I'm passionate about serving others to become better versions of themselves. I work hard to find resources for the chamber and other organizations within our influence. There is so much potential for the community and the state where I live, and my goal is to make that potential more visible and develop it. Ideas constantly flow into my head; no matter how hard I try, I cannot rest. Once one project is complete, I replace it with another. To this day, I tell people things are beginning to calm down for me, but it's just another way of saying, "Now that things are slowing down, my mind has more capacity to think about other projects that need attention." God granted me these gifts, and the only way I feel satisfied is by using my gifts on a regular basis.

PASSION

As the chamber began its massive growth spurt, people started to ask why and how I do it. I didn't know it was my passion until these last few years. I started to reflect on the chamber's achievements, my own achievements, and what the end game was going to look like for me. Passion was the only reason how I was getting things done. It was the main driver, and it continued to push me even when I didn't want to at times. I became passionate about changing the current narrative of Black Utah, the challenges the community was experiencing, and the feeling that not enough was getting done. Once I began to realize the impact I was making and the potential to do more, I finally accepted my passion.

PASSION IS A SOFT SKILL

While working at the bank, one of my bosses shared with me that some soft skills just can't be taught. He was confident that he could teach his position to me. He knew he could pass his knowledge to me. He thought that one day, I would be his successor. The ability to build relationships and connect with people in the way I do is one of my biggest strengths, an ability that would be one of the most important abilities in this role. Soft skills are deeply rooted in people's personalities and related to their habits and life experiences, whereas hard skills are more task-oriented and can be taught more easily. What is the most important soft skill in living with purpose? Your passion. People can feel your passion, and it's contagious. If you're hanging out with someone who is passionate, you can't help but want to be engaged in whatever they're doing. The energy they create becomes shared with everyone around them. There's more happiness and optimism. Passion, combined with other soft skills, gives you a competitive edge. Think about your soft skills and how you can build on them. Think about a time you were passionate about something. How did everyone around you respond? How did you use the energy of others to accomplish your goals?

INFLUENCE

Passion draws out your leadership ability. It's impossible not to influence others when you are passionate. Your energy, enthusiasm, and ambition that come from your passion attract people to you. Passion influences. My influence didn't come from wanting to be a leader. My influence came from my passion. The ability to connect with people, have a vision, and solve problems are all qualities of my leadership, but they were all birthed out of my passion. Vice versa, the strongest leaders are those that are passionate. I feel it's hard to follow a leader who doesn't lead with passion. How do you measure their commitment? Are they happy with the role they have? Think about a non-passionate leader you may have had in your life. How influential were they to you? Most likely, not much at all.

CHECKMATE

"Leadership is influence. Nothing more, nothing less."

— JOHN MAXWELL

It took me a while to understand how I influence others. I prefer leading from the front rather than in the back. I am not afraid to get my hands dirty, leading by example and showing people how it can be done. That was my style in the beginning, and once people saw the vision, I was able to pass on my activity to others, and I began to focus on my relationships in the community. I began to "build my chess board." I am not good at chess, but I consider myself pretty strong at the chess of life. People within your network can represent certain pieces you need to accomplish your goals. Some are willing to be the boots on the ground by volunteering or making introductions. As you grow your influence, you will attract people who have a larger network and more experience to be your ally and a connector. The larger your influence, the more diverse your network will become so you can build out a solid strategy for your purpose. You can identify your bishops, rooks, and knights who can make certain moves to support you. Over this last year, as I began to transition out of leading the chamber, I have been very strategic in how I have been building my team. It became more than just needing as many hands as I could get. I have specific needs that require specific qualities, skills, and experience, and I search in my network to identify those people. I have a whole process I go through to determine how people will play a role in my overall vision. Think about your network. Who can you identify in your influence that can play a role on your chess board?

ENDURANCE

Life is going to give you life. Meaning everything that life offers, the good, bad, and the ugly, is going to come your way. It's never going to be perfect. It will never be fair. You will make mistakes. You will fail sometimes. And guess what? That's supposed to happen. If you want the easy life, taking the path of least resistance, what do you think that will give you? Most likely, not what you desire. We all want the most out of life, but what are we willing to do to get it? Any life with purpose will not be easy. It's going to challenge you. It's going to test you. You have to be willing to endure it all. Staying passionate requires growth: physically, mentally, emotionally, and spiritually. The most successful people in life are the ones who are solving the biggest problems. They are living out their full purpose in life. But it required a lot of strength in all aspects of their being.

YOUR WHY

A mentor once told me, "If your why doesn't make you cry, it's not strong enough." A strong enough purpose will keep you going when the going gets tough. It will make you want to find ways to overcome life's obstacles because you want it so badly. Don't let life's struggles win. Think about what you can do to grow your endurance. Do you have a daily routine that keeps you strong? Who do you turn to when things get hard, and you need answers? When was the last time you checked in with yourself? To go all the way, you need your endurance to grow.

Passion will only take you so far. Your network can support your external needs, but how can you make sure your internal needs are supported?

WHAT'S NEXT?

I've had an amazing experience building the Utah Black Chamber and the other organizations, but my goal is never to lead any of them forever. I was just focused on solutions to the problems the community has been experiencing and having a passion for working on them. Now the goal is the succession plan. How do I establish a solid foundation for each organization to prepare it for the next leader and identify the right person to lead? That is the true test for me. The ultimate measurement of my leadership is to not only replace me in my roles, but also to help build those leaders to have a solid succession plan as well. We have heard the quote, "Feed a man fish, feed him for a day, teach a man to fish, feed him for a lifetime." But how about, teach a man to teach his children how to fish and end world hunger? That's legacy. No one should ever feel stuck in a role, especially when it comes to a role in a community. Many of us start these organizations out of passion but have a hard time moving on from it. Sometimes it's hard to move on from something you love, even when you are struggling with the energy or time to commit. I have seen several organizations struggle after their leader moved on because the leader moved on before preparing the organization for the next chapter. Those leaders left because they were tired or lost their passion, change within the people or the community began to push them away, they were moving, had accepted another role, or they simply didn't care enough for the organization to continue, so it died along with them leaving.

Many organizations end up closing or struggling to stay open, and others took several years before they got back on their feet. Don't turn your passion into an obligation. Some people will allow a role in their organization to define who they are, which makes it even more challenging to leave. I thought I would feel this same way when I left the chamber. I stayed on for a year to assist with the transition and remained behind the scenes. I still attend events, but I don't take any part in the planning. Sometimes, I do find myself wanting to help out, but I know this is not part of the plan. I have to be willing to let go, so the Black Chamber can learn how to sustain and grow without my support. I see the chamber as one of my own children. Eventually, it has to learn how to live a life independently, but I will always be there when I am in need. Anytime staff from the chamber reaches out to me, it's because of a process that hasn't been fully transitioned from me. Other than that, I want to see it thrive. I want it to become bigger and better. More and more, I am able to step away from the responsibilities and see its new leadership continue to elevate the organization. This is why purpose is so important. Allow your passion and goals to be led by your purpose. If you focus on your purpose, you'll make the moves necessary to ensure the organization can carry on after you have left. God willing, I am grateful to see the chamber continue its growth for decades.

Now I have time to finish building a path for the Black Chamber Foundation, Black Success Center, Living Color Utah, and the programming for youth. I can focus on growing my business and developing more leaders around me. The more leaders around me focused on the vision, the more time I can focus on other projects still on the shelf. When you have a purpose as big as mine, the passion will keep me moving.

The work doesn't have to stop locally, either. Opportunities for my purpose exist in every part of this country and possibly the world. I have developed some great relationships with influencers in other states and am looking forward to sharing my purpose and working together to identify opportunities to expand in their marketplace. Utah will always be home, but what I've built here can also be a template for other states to use.

FINAL THOUGHTS

I hope you took the time to reflect at the end of each chapter. While I have opened up and shared my story with you, I hope my experiences and thoughts have inspired you to think about your experiences, goals, the people around you, and what you are trying to accomplish. Did this help you identify what purpose you are serving here on Earth? Do you have a list of things that you are passionate about? Now it's time to make a plan. If it brings purpose and happiness to your life, It's never too late to design what the rest of your life is going to look like. You are a light to the world, and it is waiting for you to shine.

"To live with purpose, find your passion, grow your influence, and maximize your endurance."

ACKNOWLEDGMENTS

I didn't realize how much courage it would take for me to write this book. While the purpose of this book was to inspire, it required me to become vulnerable in sharing my story. This book stretched my comfort zone, and I am grateful for this journey I decided to take. It was not easy, and I could not have done it without the support of some very important people.

Michelle, I love you. Thank you for your unwavering support. My laptop has constantly been literally on my lap more than you would like to see it in the evenings, but you supported me throughout not only this whole process but all the community engagements I committed myself to. You are more than my partner in life; you are also my first board member, a partner in the community, and even a co-worker. You are amazing, and I thank you for being a part of this journey and helping me become the person I am today.

To my children, Zoe, Memphis, and Audrie. Thank you for always inspiring me to keep going. You may not even know how much you keep me going, but I work hard to be an example for you. I appreciate all of your support and love.

Mom and Dad, thank you for providing me with a strong foundation and for being my cheerleaders. I always want to make you proud and show everyone how great of a son you have. I love you as well, sis!

To the Utah Black Chamber leadership from the beginning to now. You all have been amazing. Melinda Anderson, Muriel Lee, Chris Adams, and John Asher, my first board members who took a chance on me to figure out how to grow this organization. To Steven Johnson, Mikell Brown, and Elle Solomon for expanding my vision of what this chamber could be and becoming good friends. Thank you so much. And to our current chamber and nonprofit board members, thank you for carrying the vision forward. I appreciate all the work you are doing.

To Dr. Sidni Lloyd-Shorter, thank you for your leadership of the chamber and the community. Thank you for taking a chance on this community and recognizing its potential to become something special.

Deonn Henderson, thank you for your belief as well. You travel back and forth from the east coast to us because you know what we can do. I appreciate you lending your wisdom and committing your time to our growth.

To Kayleigh O'Keefe and the Soul Excellence Team. Thank you for believing in me and partnering with me on this opportunity. This has been an amazing experience, and I'm excited about our relationship and where we can go next!

To my village. Calvary Baptist Church and Pastor Emeritus, Rev. France Davis, thank you for being a part of raising me. Your love and support are one of the main reasons why I am the person I am today. Robert Rendon and the original founders of the Utah Hispanic Chamber, Sergio Palacio, Art Pina, and former President Francisco Sotelo, thank you for your belief in me, your mentorship, and your support. Special shout out to Kazua Pferdner, my manager at Morgan Stanley, who pushed to elevate my game, and President & CEO of Zions Bank, Scott Anderson, and Zions Bank for the opportunities you have given me and the support of the Utah Black Chamber and community. To the other diverse chambers of commerce and diverse business organizations within Living Color Utah, business resource partners, and all the chamber members, thank you for believing in the vision of what this community will be and our partnership. Dajon Young, you opened a door and didn't realize it would be all this behind it! Thanks for inviting me to be your business partner. What a fun time we had!

Michael Styles, I know you're in heaven smiling down, saying, "I told you so!" Thank you for believing in me. I don't appreciate you leaving me hanging, but I know you didn't mean to. Knowing you, you already knew that I didn't need much of your help other than a little encouragement. Thanks, man.

Papa, I miss you and love you. Thank you for everything you did for me – your love, encouragement, humor, and your example. Thank you for paving the way for your grandson. I bet you saw all this coming!

PLAYLIST

James Jackson III's
Living with Purpose Playlist
Apple Music
Spotify

1. *Golden* – Jill Scott
2. *Thank You (feat. Big Sean)* – DJ Khaled
3. *Anthem (Soundtrack Version)* – Dreamville, Big Sean & EST Gee
4. *Ultra Black (feat. Hit-Boy)* – Nas
5. *I'm Going All the Way* – Sounds of Blackness
6. *It's Goin' Down (feat. Nitti)* – Young Joc
7. *Strictly Business* – LL Cool J
8. *For the Love of Money* – O'Jays
9. *Juicy* – The Notorious B.I.G.
10. *Michelle* – The Beatles
11. *We Gonna Make It (feat. Styles P)* – Jadakiss
12. *Hustlin'* – Rick Ross
13. *Umma Do Me* – Rocko

14. *Can't Stop, Won't Stop (feat. Chingy)* – Young Gunz
15. *Legacy* – Jay-Z
16. *Legacy* – Mike Posner & Talib Kweli
17. *Moment of Clarity* – Jay-Z
18. *Steak Um (feat. ScHoolboy Q)* – Black Thought
19. *I Smile* – Kirk Franklin
20. *Set Me Free (feat. YK Osiris)* – Lecrae
21. *One Sixteen (feat. KB & Andy Mineo)* – Trip Lee

James Jackson, III is a community builder.

James Jackson, III currently serves as the Supplier Diversity Program Manager at Zions Bancorporation where he is responsible for building relationships with capable diverse suppliers who can provide goods and services across the enterprise. Mr. Jackson has worked in various areas of the financial industry for 20 years and found his passion in serving and building his community. In conjunction with his role at the bank, Mr. Jackson has served or currently serves on many boards of directors, such as Big Brothers Big Sisters of Utah, the Economic Development Corporation of Utah, and the State Workforce Development Board to name a few.

In 2009, he founded the Utah Black Chamber. The Chamber was formed to serve the needs of the Black business community and has since become known for connecting and growing Utah's Black community. Because of its influence, the organization has doubled in size year over year in the last five years, and it continues to expand its platform with a business incubator and a Black history museum coming in the next few years. In 2022, Mr. Jackson stepped down as the President & CEO to focus on other projects and organizations to elevate Utah's diverse community, such as Living Color Utah and the Utah Diversity Career Fair.

Mr. Jackson is a bestselling author, speaker, and trainer focused on helping people everywhere live with purpose. He has also been a frequent contributor to the *Utah Business Magazine* where he writes about diversity and leadership. At the end of 2020, Mr. Jackson, along with 24 business leaders around the world authored the book, *Leading Through the Pandemic: Unconventional Wisdom from Heartfelt Leaders*. At the beginning of 2022, Mr. Jackson facilitated the Utah Black Chamber's book publication, *Black Utah: Stories from a Thriving Community*, featuring interviews with dozens of changemakers in Utah.

Mr. Jackson was honored as Utah Business Magazine's Forty under 40 (2020), Westminster College's Unsung Hero (2018), and Omega Psi Phi Citizen of the Year (2018). He also was presented with the Dr. Ronald G. Coleman Alumni Award and the David Eccles School of Business Rising Star Award from the University of Utah in 2023. In the spring of 2022, he earned his Diversity and Inclusion Certification from Cornell University. He earned his undergraduate degree from the University of Utah in 2002 and his MBA from the University of Phoenix in 2010.

As a Utah native, Mr. James Jackson, III is committed to the social and economic growth of the state's Black and overall diverse community. His goal is to further promote Utah's diversity with the hopes of it becoming a more attractive destination for people of color. He and Michelle Crawford have been together since 2009 and have three children, Zoe, Memphis, and Audrie, and their dog, Max.

http://j3motivation.com

facebook.com/james3motivation
instagram.com/j3motivation
linkedin.com/in/jamesjacksoniii

Black Utah: Stories from a Thriving Community. This book highlights the stories and experiences of the Black Community living in Utah. It contains dozens of interviews from diverse individuals sharing why Utah has a community for them and how they are thriving in this increasingly dynamic corner of the Mountain West.

Soul Excellence Publishing, 2022

———

Leading Through the Pandemic: Unconventional Wisdom from Heartfelt Leaders. With conscious leaders showing the way, this book outlines the leadership lessons they don't teach you in business school and provides a new blueprint for 21st-century leadership.

Should Excellence Publishing, 2021

NOTES

2. THE VILLAGE

1. Olin, Andy. 2021. "There Are Only 19 Prosperous Majority-Black Zip Codes in the US. the Houston Area Is Home to Two." Kinder Institute for Urban Research | Rice University. January 13. https://kinder.rice.edu/urbanedge/there-are-only-19-prosperous-majority-black-zip-codes-us-houston-area-home-two.

12. ENDURANCE: CAN'T STOP, WON'T STOP

1. Suni, Eric. 2021. "How Much Sleep Do We Really Need?" Sleep Foundation. March 9, 2021. https://www.sleepfoundation.org/how-sleep-works/how-much-sleep-do-we-really-need.

15. ENDURANCE: TAKE CARE OF YOU

1. "Exclusive Interview with Lecrae." 2016. The Wheaton Record. February 18, 2016. https://thewheatonrecord.com/2016/02/18/exclusive-interview-with-lecrae/.